The Power of the Agile Business Analyst

30 *surprising* ways a business analyst can add value to your Agile development team

The Power of the Agile Business Analyst

30 *surprising* ways a business analyst can add value to your Agile development team

JAMIE LYNN COOKE

IT Governance Publishing

IT Governance Publishing
IT Governance Limited
Unit 3, Clive Court
Bartholomew's Walk
Cambridgeshire Business Park
Ely
Cambridgeshire
CB7 4EA
United Kingdom

www.itgovernance.co.uk

First published in the United Kingdom in 2013
by IT Governance Publishing.

ISBN 978-1-84928-504-9

DEDICATION

To my mother, Sheila, for her unconditional love and her relentless pursuit of seven-letter Scrabble™ words.

FOREWORD

Agile has been misquoted, misused, and downright abused by commercial interests. And now we hear that Agile has negated the need for documentation; that Agile speeds up development by months or even years; and, if only we all used it, then world peace would reign.

The challenge (or one of the major challenges…) of Agile is to make sure that it is properly understood, that wild claims about 'no more documentation' or 'development cycles reduced to days rather than months' - or any of the myriad countless and baseless claims made about Agile being some form of magic - are countered by *practical, achievable approaches* before expectations get out of control. This book does all of that and more. Not only is it one of the best books about Agile that I have read, it is one of the best books about ANY good practices that I have read.

It is more than refreshing to find an author who knows the subject inside out, provides direct, clear guidance, and, probably most important, reinforces the fact that good practices still require intelligent and pragmatic application.

If there is any justice, Agile will not be burdened with unfeasible expectations, and books such as this will reinforce the excellence of the concepts and their practical application; and hopefully establish Jamie Lynn Cooke as a genuine authority in the domain.

I look forward to the next book!

Brian Johnson, CA.

PREFACE

Agile approaches empower development teams to deliver the *greatest business-value software solutions* that can be achieved within the time, resourcing, and budget constraints of each project. These approaches focus the Agile team members on building the highest-priority features, on replacing reams of documentation with face-to-face communication, on identifying (and addressing) risks as early as possible in the project timeline, and on continuously reviewing and adapting the developed solution to meet the ongoing needs of the business.

One of the core strategies to achieve these objectives is encouraging the Agile development team to work *as closely as possible* with business users throughout the project timeline. This ongoing interaction enables the Agile developers to better understand the business users' requirements and priorities, reduces their mutual dependence on written specifications, focuses the development team on continually delivering the highest-priority capabilities in the software, and confirms the delivered solution genuinely meets the needs of the business.

Although specific Agile methods, such as Scrum, XP®, Lean, and DSDM, differ in their approaches to delivering high business-value solutions, each of these methods equips the Agile developers with practices and tools that are designed to increase the quality, relevance, and extensibility of the software that the team delivers. The Agile community, as a whole, also provides developers with countless supporting resources, including books, websites, forums, and conferences where Agile development issues can be raised, discussed, and jointly addressed by the group.

The interesting thing is that, where Agile approaches go to great lengths to provide the developers with the foundation they need to deliver high-value software solutions, there is *relatively little* equivalent support provided for the business users. In most Agile methods, the business user is *solely responsible* for the identification, requirements gathering, clarification, and assignment of priorities for the requested system capabilities. These methods generally work from the assumption that the business users have separately collaborated with all the relevant stakeholders prior to each joint planning session, and that their collective input is accurately represented. Agile methods also assume the business users have sufficient knowledge, vision, and objectivity to ensure the capabilities they are requesting represent the best possible solution for the organization. Likewise, Agile methods anticipate that the business users will be *available* throughout the project to provide the Agile developers with accurate and timely ongoing feedback. Although the intention of having Agile development teams working directly with business areas throughout the project is a noble one, without a reasonable level of support for the business users, the execution can fall short.

One of the biggest challenges for Agile projects is when business users have limited (or no) availability to spend significant time working with the Agile development team, due to the commitments of their primary roles. Although these business users may be available at the very beginning of an iteration (for initial requirements discussions and planning) and at the very end of an iteration (for system walkthroughs and retrospectives), what happens when the Agile team needs business input at other points in the development process?

Another less apparent, but equally significant challenge, is when the requested capabilities and priorities provided by the business users are based too heavily on their current work, without having *objectively* considered the potential efficiencies a new solution (and corresponding business process improvements) could provide.

Similar questions can arise about the value of the business users' requested capabilities in an Agile solution when they have not consulted with the *full range* of stakeholders who will be impacted by the solution, or when they have insufficient background information on the policy, regulatory, or technical constraints of the solution to truly understand the overhead costs of implementing these capabilities.

All of these situations can significantly compromise the collaboration between the business users and the Agile development team. This not only has implications for the business value of the delivered solution (and the perception of the Agile team) but also impacts ongoing project funding and, potentially, jeopardizes future support for Agile approaches in the organization altogether. No matter how effective Agile approaches are in delivering production-ready software, the real measures of success are the *quality*, *relevance*, and *business value* of the implemented solution.

The Power of the Agile Business Analyst: *30 surprising ways a business analyst can add value to your Agile development team* challenges whether Agile projects are truly positioned to deliver the highest-value business solutions without offering business users the equivalent level of support, validation, and collaboration that is provided for the Agile development team. If Agile projects are designed to deliver the greatest business-value software solution that can be achieved, why would the business users not get an equivalent level of support for their work?

To address this challenge, ***The Power of the Agile Business Analyst*** proposes including an Agile business analyst on the development team to provide business users with the support they need, as well as a valuable resource to assist Agile developers in their analysis, design, testing, and implementation work throughout the project.

Most importantly, ***The Power of the Agile Business Analyst*** details 30 core activities the Agile business analyst can undertake to ensure the business users and Agile developers deliver the highest business-value solution for the organization, and guides you in identifying the most critical subset of Agile business analyst activities for the specific needs of your project.

ABOUT THE AUTHOR

Jamie Lynn Cooke has 22 years of experience as a senior business analyst and solutions consultant, working with more than 130 public and private sector organizations throughout Australia, Canada, and the United States.

Her background includes business case development; strategic and operational reviews; business process modeling, mapping, and optimization; product and project management on small to multi-million dollar initiatives; quality management; risk analysis and mitigation; developing/conducting training courses; workshop delivery; and refining e-business strategies.

She is the author of *Agile Principles Unleashed*, a book written specifically to explain Agile in non-technical business terms to managers and executives outside of the IT industry; *Agile: An Executive Guide: Real results from IT budgets*, which gives IT executives the tools and strategies needed for bottom-line business decisions on using Agile methodologies; and *Everything you want to know about Agile: How to get Agile results in a less-than-Agile organization*, which gives readers strategies for aligning Agile work within the reporting, budgeting, staffing, and governance constraints of their organization.

She is a well-regarded speaker on both business and technology topics, most recently presenting on issues such as *Getting Management and Business User Support for Using Agile* and *When is Agile Not the Answer?* at the Business Process Modelling world conference in Brisbane, Australia and at the AgileCanberra professional forums.

About the author

Jamie has been working hands-on with Agile methodologies since 2003, and has researched hundreds of books and articles on Agile topics. She is a signatory to the Agile Manifesto, has attended numerous Agile seminars, and has worked with prominent consultants to promote Agile methodologies to large organizations.

Jamie has a Bachelor of Science in Engineering Psychology (Human Factors Engineering) from Tufts University in Medford, Massachusetts; and a Graduate Certificate in e-Business/Business Informatics from the University of Canberra in Australia.

ACKNOWLEDGEMENTS

My continued thanks to the pioneers and thought leaders of the Agile world, most notably Kent Beck, Martin Fowler, Alistair Cockburn, Jeff Sutherland, Mike Cohn, Ken Schwaber, and Jim Highsmith, for their passionate work in developing and refining Agile methodologies over the past two decades. Particular thanks go to Artem Marchenko of AgileSoftwareDevelopment.com[1] for generously making his tracking tools available for everyone in the Agile community to use.

Thanks also to the small and large organizations worldwide that have shared their Agile experiences, including Nokia Siemens Networks, Yahoo!, Google, Microsoft®, and BT.

Special thanks to Neil Salkind of the Salkind Literary Agency and Vicki Utting of IT Governance Publishing for their ongoing support and sage advice. Thanks also to Chris Evans, ITSM Specialist and ir. H.L. (Maarten) Souw RE, Enterprise Risk and QA Manager, UWV, for their helpful comments during the review process.

Many thanks, as well, to the people who taught me the most about the strategies of the business world over the past 22 years, especially Roland Scornavacca, Tony Robey, and Peter Walsh; to Rowan Bunning for being an unending source of Agile knowledge; and to the writers and teachers who inspired me, particularly Richard Leonard[2] for his

---

1 *www.AgileSoftwareDevelopment.com.*

2 Richard Leonard's website: *richardleonard.net.*

amazing ability to encourage writers with his humor and enthusiasm.

Finally, my eternal gratitude to my parents, my US family, my Australian family, and my friends, most especially Michele, Susan, Linda, Elissa, and Janice, for continuing to be my sanity check in this world. Most of all, thank you to my husband, David, for 21 years of love and laughter.

CONTENTS

INTRODUCTION

Not all Agile development teams – or all business users – are equal.

In an ideal world, the business users who work with the Agile development team would be intimately familiar with the requirements of every business area impacted by the delivered solution (and the relative priority of each requested capability); they would be objective enough to see the solution beyond their current work practices; and they would fully understand the policy, regulatory, and technical constraints of every feature in the solution. In this perfect scenario, the business users would also be *continually available* to work with the development team throughout the project timeline to investigate their questions, to provide real-time feedback on the system capabilities in progress, to resolve any conflicting input from stakeholders (and management), and to prepare the intended users – and the organization overall – for upcoming software releases.

Conversely, the Agile development team may find themselves working with business users who have extremely limited availability to work with the team, who have just enough knowledge of the business requirements to be dangerous, or who insist on single-handedly making decisions on behalf of the organization, all of which can significantly reduce the accuracy, relevance, and value of the delivered solution.

For most Agile projects, including yours, the business users who work with the Agile developers fall somewhere in the spectrum between these two extremes (hopefully leaning more toward the ideal model!). There will, however, come a time in every Agile project when even the most well-intentioned business users will be unavailable to give the Agile developers real-time answers to their questions, to provide feedback on the software in progress, or to investigate and resolve the outstanding business issues raised during development. Equally, there will be times when the business users need input from other areas of the organization, but do not have the availability (or the resources) to follow through in the time-frames needed by the development team.

So what does the Agile development team do when the business users have limited (or no) availability to provide the input needed to progress project work? Do they escalate the issue to management to find a replacement (or supplemental) business representative, who may not agree with the original business users' requirements and priorities? Do they put the development work (or the unresolved portion of the work) on hold until the original business users are available? Do they make decisions on behalf of the business users, in the hope that any incorrect assumptions (and the resulting development work) will be addressed in the next iterative review session?

This 'holding pattern' situation is one of the many risks of having *individual, unsupported business users* as the sole point of business information, prioritization, and issue resolution for the Agile solution; and it is one of the strongest arguments for including an Agile business analyst on the project team.

Having an Agile business analyst on the project team not only provides the Agile developers with an alternative, more readily available source when business knowledge is needed but also provides the business users with ongoing support for their activities throughout the project timeline, making them more available to work with the Agile developers on the most critical review and decision activities at each point. These are only two of the many ways in which an Agile business analyst can add significant value to the Agile team – and the delivered solution.

The Power of the Agile Business Analyst details 30 activities that Agile business analysts can undertake throughout the project timeline to substantially increase the relevance, quality, usability, and overall business value of the delivered solution, including:

- quantifying the business case for the developed solution, and providing valuation of individual software features
- encouraging business users to think beyond their 'business as usual' activities
- helping business users to articulate their requirements
- identifying the full spectrum of options for addressing business requirements beyond the software solution, including:
  - business process improvements,
  - targeted staff training,
  - restructuring of roles, and
  - more effective corporate communication
- challenging business users when their requested software features may not deliver the level of business value they anticipate
- researching the data migration, systems integration, security, and capacity requirements of the solution
- acting on behalf of the business user during software implementation, including the development and

execution of acceptance tests, creation of documentation, and provision of training

- providing expertise on aligning user interfaces, supporting documentation, and training materials to the needs of each target audience.

This book has been written specifically to provide you with everything you need to leverage the skills, opportunities, and value an Agile business analyst can add to your Agile project team:

Chapter 1: What is Agile? provides a high-level overview of what Agile approaches are, who uses them, and the most common Agile methods in use.

Chapter 2: The Power and the Perils of Agile identifies the limitations in current Agile approaches that can affect the business value of your delivered solution.

Chapter 3: Why Your Team Needs an Agile Business Analyst introduces the discussion on how including a skilled business analyst can add significant value to your Agile team.

Chapter 4: What are the Risks of Not Having an Agile Business Analyst? describes key issues that can arise when business users do not receive the same level of support as developers on an Agile project.

Chapter 5: 30 Ways for the Agile Business Analyst to Add Value to Your Project details 30 specific activities the Agile business analyst can do to assist the business users and the Agile developers throughout the project.

Chapter 6: Getting the Right Agile Business Analyst for Your Team provides you with guidelines on how to hire the right Agile business analyst for your team. It also offers guidance for those business analysts who have previously worked on waterfall software development projects to transition their skills to Agile projects.

Chapter 7: Moving Your Agile Team Forward helps you to identify where an Agile business analyst can provide the most value for your specific project needs.

Chapter 8: More Information on Agile provides general and practice-specific Agile and business analysis resources that you can refer to for further information.

At the end of this book is an *Author's Note on Agile Business Analysis Resources*, explaining why there are relatively few resources currently available on this topic, and how you can share your ideas, questions, and concerns with the Agile community.

CHAPTER 1: WHAT IS AGILE?[1]

'Agile' is a collective term for methodologies (and practices) that have emerged over the past two decades to increase the relevance, quality, flexibility, and business value of software solutions. These *adaptive management* approaches are specifically intended to address the problems that have historically plagued software development and service delivery activities in the IT industry, including budget overruns, missed deadlines, low-quality outputs, and dissatisfied users.

Although there is a broad range of Agile methodologies in the IT industry – from software development and project delivery approaches to strategies for software maintenance – all Agile methodologies share the same basic objectives:

- To *replace upfront planning with incremental planning* that adapts to the most current information available ('Apply, Inspect, Adapt').
- To *minimize the impact of changing requirements* by providing a low overhead structure to accommodate variations to the originally identified requirements throughout the project.
- To *build in quality upfront* and then relentlessly confirm the integrity of the solution throughout the process.

---

1 For those who follow this author's writing, some of the introductory material from *Everything You Want to Know about Agile: How to get Agile results in a less-than-Agile organization*, Jamie Lynn Cooke, IT Governance Publishing (2012) has been adapted for use in this book, serving the same purpose as in the original.

- To *address technical risks as early in the process as possible* to reduce the potential for cost and time blowouts as the project progresses.
- To *entrust and empower staff* to continuously deliver high business-value outputs.
- To *provide frequent and continuous business value to the organization* by focusing staff on regularly delivering the highest-priority features in the solution as fully functional, fully tested, production-ready capabilities.
- To *encourage ongoing communication between the business areas and project team members* to increase the relevance, usability, quality, and acceptance of delivered solutions.

> **Agile methodologies** are common-sense approaches for applying the finite resources of an organization to continuously deliver low risk, high business-value software solutions

The last two bullet points in this list cannot be emphasized enough. Where traditional waterfall software development projects focus on using extensive upfront documentation to detail user requirements before development work can even begin, Agile approaches rely on *shared communication* between the development team and the business users throughout the project, with the business users' highest priority requested features regularly presented to them as *fully functional software* to confirm whether or not the delivered solution meets their requirements.

Some of the most common Agile methodologies (also referred to as 'Agile Methods') include:

- iterative strategies for managing software development projects, such as Scrum, Dynamic Systems

Development Method (DSDM), Feature-Driven Development (FDD™), the Agile Unified Process (AUP), and Lean Development

- strategies for optimizing software development work, such as eXtreme Programming (XP™) and the Rational Unified Process (RUP)
- strategies for managing software maintenance and support activities, such as Kanban.

These Agile methodologies have been (and continue to be) successfully used by thousands of organizations worldwide[2], most notably in the United States and Europe. Some of the more prominent organizations using Agile methodologies include Nokia Siemens Networks[3], Yahoo![4], Google[5], Microsoft®[6], BT[7], Bankwest[8], SunCorp[9], and Wells Fargo[10].

---

2 As evidenced by the number of signatories to the Agile Manifesto (*Agilemanifesto.org*) as at June 2013

3 NokiaSiemens and Agile Development, Haapio P, JAOO (2008): *http://jaoo.dk/file?path=/jaoo-aarhus-2008/slides//PetriHaapio_CanAGLobalCompany.pdf.*

4 Lessons from a Yahoo Scrum Rollout, Mackie K (2008): *http://campustechnology.com/articles/2008/02/lessons-from-a-yahoo-scrum-rollout.aspx.*

5 Scaling Scrum & Distributed Teams – Scrum Tuning: Lessons Learned at Google, Sutherland J (2006): *youtube.com/watch?v=WUQfuhdOZ8s.*

6 Microsoft Lauds Scrum Method for Software Projects, Taft D K (2005): *eweek.com/c/a/IT-Management/Microsoft-Lauds-Scrum-Method-for-Software-Projects/.*

7 Agile Coaching in British Telecom, Meadows L and Hanly S (2006): *Agilejournal.com/articles/columns/column-articles/144-Agile-coaching-in-british-telecom.*

---

8 Bankwest goes Agile: project time slashed, Braue D (2010): *zdnet.com/bankwest-goes-Agile-project-time-slashed-1339306091/.*

9 Suncorp goes Agile for 19k desktop integration project (2008): *itnews.com.au/News/130927,suncorp-goes-Agile-for-19k-desktop-integration-project.aspx.*

10 Is Agile Development Only for Nerds?, Matta E (2008): *http://radiowalker.wordpress.com/2008/10/07/is-Agile-development-only-for-nerds/.*

CHAPTER 2: THE POWER AND THE PERILS OF AGILE

The ability for Agile approaches to deliver real results is both its greatest strength and its greatest exposure. Organizations often get so excited about the effectiveness of Agile approaches that they become complacent to its perils.

For organizations that have been burned by historical failures in their IT projects, the ability to receive *working software* on a *regular basis* can be refreshing, almost enchanting. Management and staff tend to see Agile as the 'cure-all' for what has historically plagued the software industry. They are often so excited by the tangible outputs of their Agile software projects that they do not stop to consider where these approaches may be lacking.

The lopsided process diagram

The following diagram shows the process used in a common Agile method (Scrum) to transition the high-level requirements identified by the business users (referred to as Product Owners) into prioritized functions that are implemented by the Agile development team:

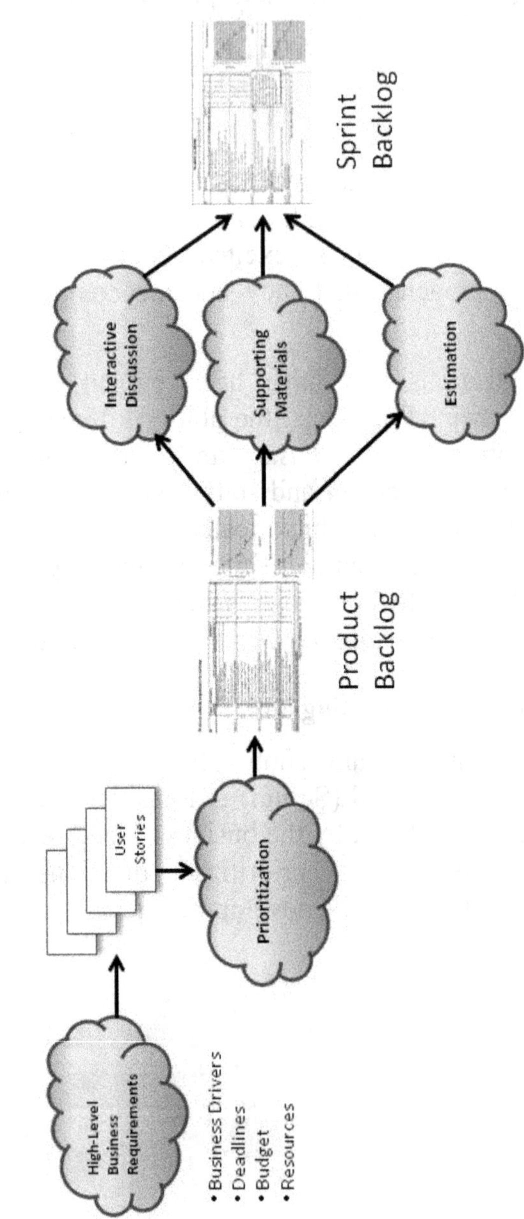

Figure 1: The lopsided process diagram

The focus of this diagram is on the activities undertaken to translate the high-level business requirements identified by the business users into *actionable functions* that the development team can work on in the upcoming iteration. In particular, the diagram shows the importance of using a *prioritized list of requested features* (the Product Backlog) as the basis for *interactive discussion and clarification* with the Agile team. The Agile team then uses the requirements information (and any supporting materials) provided by the business users to estimate the amount of effort required to deliver each requested feature. The objective is to produce an agreed list of system capabilities that the Agile development team believes can be achieved in the upcoming iteration (the Sprint Backlog).

The irony is that this one diagram equally shows some of the greatest strengths and the greatest weaknesses in Agile methods.

The right-hand side of this diagram depicts the ScrumMaster, Scrum Team Members and Product Owner's use of *interactive discussion*, *supporting materials*, and *estimation* to establish a shared understanding of what the business users require and what the Agile team can reasonably achieve. These tasks are well understood in the Agile community, including numerous resources, tools, and techniques (e.g. *Planning Poker*[1]) that are available to support these activities.

The left-hand side of this diagram, however, depicts one of the greatest weaknesses in Agile methods: the *undefined* and *unstructured* way in which the Product Owner (i.e. the

---

1 See *planningpoker.com* for further details on this technique.

business users) translate their high-level requirements into user stories and how they then assign priorities to these stories.

In many Agile projects, business users are left on their own to make these decisions. The Agile team only becomes involved in the process at the point in which the prioritized list is brought to the table for discussion, which means the Agile team members are relying almost exclusively on the business users to accurately reflect the needs and the priorities of all business areas.

The challenge is that most business users are highly familiar with what *their area* of the business does, often coming from the perspective of how a new (or replacement) software solution could make *their current work* easier. Rarely, however, do they have the insight (or time) to consider where their current business processes are lacking, where work could be done more efficiently, or even where a software solution is not the only answer to their business problems.

Some Agile proponents will argue that it is not exclusively the role of the business users to compile the initial set of user stories and bring them to the team. They encourage the business users to work collaboratively with the Agile development team (e.g. in a workshop session) at the start of each project to scope the solution and to identify all the known user stories (even if they are only known at a very high level).

Although this approach can provide support – and a sounding board – for the business user, it still depends upon the business users having an accurate understanding of what the system needs to deliver and knowing the relative importance of each requested feature. It also depends on the business users having the objectivity and vision to see *beyond* the software solution to consider business process and policy changes that could better address their business needs. The Agile team can help the business users to document each of their requirements in the appropriate structure (and level of granularity) for a user story, and help them to establish realistic acceptance criteria for each user story. It is rare, however, that the Agile team is knowledgeable enough about the functions, processes, policies, resourcing levels, and skill sets of the business area to truly assess and, where needed, *challenge* each requested feature.

The fact that business users get relatively minimal support in their requirements identification and prioritization work may not, in effect, be a *peril* for an Agile project, but it can put the relevance and business value of the delivered solution at risk.

Chapter 4: What are the Risks of Not Having an Agile Business Analyst? provides further detail on the specific risks and exposures of having unsupported business users on an Agile project, including:

- basing the proposed solution exclusively on 'business as usual' processes and practices
- seeing software as the *only* solution to a business issue
- prioritizing features based on preference, not business value
- not having the time (or resources) to:
  - get input from all affected stakeholders
  - investigate policy or regulatory constraints
  - analyze and clean up legacy data
  - coordinate cross-organizational communication

    - secure necessary project funding, for example, for upgrading servers
- being stuck in development, acceptance testing, or implementation 'holding patterns' when individual business users are unavailable to work with the Agile team.

The remaining chapters of this book provide you with strategies and activities to help you overcome these risks.

The slippery slope

Many other perils can impact the success of Agile projects, including:

- technical constraints, such as legacy systems, bundled systems, and third-party products that limit the Agile team's ability to use incremental delivery approaches
- restrictions in current contractual arrangements that make it difficult (if not impossible) to support Agile approaches
- senior managers who do not endorse the use of these approaches
- an organizational culture that does not encourage collaboration and open communication (for example, an organization that rewards silo-building and personal recognition over teamwork)
- project frameworks that require too much upfront documentation and pre-authorization of scoped work to support emergent requirements.

All of these represent real challenges that can not only reduce the value of the delivered solution, they can stop the Agile project before it even begins. The interesting thing is that an issue which stops an Agile project from proceeding altogether may actually be *less of a risk* to Agile success than an issue that allows the Agile project to continue with *unnoticed risks*.

When an organization invests in the development of a software solution, it is generally based on the expectation that the delivered solution will result in *net gains* for the organization, such as:

- reduced operational overheads
- increased profits
- faster times to market
- greater employee satisfaction
- better customer service.

Every time the Agile development team expends effort on a feature that can only benefit a small set of users, or one that supports an existing inefficient business process, or one that costs more to develop than the corresponding net gain for the organization, the overall value of the delivered solution decreases. Any one of these 'low-value' features may not be substantial enough to significantly impact the net gains provided by the software, but the cumulative total of several low-value features can devalue the overall solution.

For traditional waterfall projects, the amount of wasted effort (and low-value outputs) can be astronomical, particularly where a specification is frozen months (and even years) before the software solution is delivered.

For Agile projects, the erosion of business value is much more subtle. The excitement the organization had when the software was first delivered is replaced by the reality of using it to support day-to-day operations. If the solution does not truly represent the needs of all target user audiences, if it replicates a horribly inefficient paper-based process with a somewhat inefficient automated equivalent process, or if staff need to implement workarounds for the software when business processes are not adequately supported, the organization's perception of the delivered solution – and of the Agile project altogether – will not be positive.

Improving continuous improvement

The perils described in the previous sections may give the impression that Agile practitioners are complacent about the effectiveness of Agile approaches. Nothing could be further from the truth.

Continuous improvement is a key driver for Agile approaches. As one example, Agile projects often include *retrospectives* – dedicated times when the project team can step back, review the work that was undertaken, and collectively reflect on both the good and bad aspects of their work. The intent of the retrospective is to recognize those processes (and people) that were particularly effective, and to identify any challenges and problems that need to be addressed to improve subsequent work.

The problem is that much of the continuous improvement work undertaken by Agile teams has too narrow a focus.

Although regular review in a retrospective is a welcome change to having the project team rely upon 'business as usual' activities (or *annual* project reviews), there is a danger for these retrospective sessions to focus too much on *refining* the already agreed processes, not *challenging* their scope. For example, the Agile development team may discuss how their automated testing activities can be improved, but they are unlikely to be asking themselves whether the business user who is working with them is sufficiently objective to see beyond current business practices, or whether the features they are building may not provide the best solution to meet the business requirements of the organization.

Similarly, the Agile community is constantly endeavoring to improve both the theory and the practices of these approaches. An Internet search for 'improving Agile' alone reveals tens of thousands of articles, blogs, and forums that specifically address opportunities for improvement (and countless other commercial websites with products and services to support these activities). The challenge is that the refinement of Agile approaches tends to focus on how they can be used to better deliver *software solutions*, that is, better identification of system requirements, delivery of higher-quality code, enabling continuous integration.

Rarely do Agile teams – or the Agile community as a whole – stop to challenge how organizations calculate the budgets for software projects, how they assign a monetary value for each software feature, or the logic that business users use to prioritize their requested system capabilities in a backlog. It is often expected that the business user will undertake these activities *independently*, acquire the necessary budget, confirm requirements with all impacted stakeholders, and then represent the prioritized needs of the business in collaborative sessions with the development team. It is also expected that the business user will consider activities *beyond the software solution* in their research, such as the business process implications of the proposed software solution, user training needs, and updates to procedural manuals.

So how does an Agile team expand its continuous improvement work to include improving the level of support provided to business users? One key way to achieve this is by including a skilled Agile business analyst on the project team.

CHAPTER 3: WHY YOUR TEAM NEEDS AN AGILE BUSINESS ANALYST

The Information Technology (IT) industry does not have a standard definition for 'business analyst' that applies to all software projects. The role of the business analyst has historically ranged from writing business cases, to detailing system specifications, to testing and documenting the developed solution, and doing everything in between. With so much variation in the definition of the role of the business analyst, it is not at all surprising that people can misinterpret – and underestimate – the value that a business analyst can bring to an Agile project.

This section identifies why the perception of business analysts needs to break away from their roles on traditional waterfall project teams, and focus instead on the value that skilled business analysts bring to Agile teams.

Is pairing only for developers?

One of the primary strengths of Agile teams is that they are multidisciplinary. Agile approaches forego the traditional assignment of specific roles to each member of the team in favor of having team members collaborate to achieve whatever is most urgently required for the project, whether it is:

- designing the solution,
- coding the features,
- building the test cases,
- or writing online help manuals for the users.

This collaborative approach is one of the core strengths of Agile methodologies. It allows each team member to achieve a more well-rounded understanding of the required solution. It increases knowledge sharing and provides greater flexibility for the team to focus resources on the most critical activities. It enables teams to more readily respond to unexpected staff leave with minimal impacts on productivity. In essence, the multidisciplinary nature of Agile teams enables all team members to be *jointly responsible* for the delivery of a successful solution, not just 'their part' of the solution.

It is for this reason that all Agile team members are called 'developers' instead of being assigned a title that constrains them to delivering only one aspect of the solution (e.g. 'tester'). Included in this division of labor is the shared responsibility of team members to work directly with the business users to identify, apply, and refine their requirements in the delivered software solution.

One example of this collaborative work is the requirements identification and clarification process jointly undertaken by the business users and the Agile development team in the Scrum methodology. As noted in the previous section, Scrum begins each project iteration (Sprint) with a *sprint planning meeting*, where the Product Owner (the business user), the ScrumMaster (the facilitator), and the entire Scrum team (the developers) review the highest-priority items identified by the Product Owner, estimate the amount of work required for each feature, and agree on the subset of features that will be included in the forthcoming sprint. *Prior to this session*, the Product Owner will have prepared the user stories and listed their requirements in top-down priority order in the product backlog to focus the team (and the discussion) on the most important features in the solution. The team then works jointly with the Product Owner during the planning session to clarify these requirements, gather any supporting information, estimate the effort required to deliver each feature, and determine what subset of capabilities can reasonably be delivered in the upcoming iteration.

The interesting thing in this example is that the *Agile development team* is multidisciplinary, with each team member sharing responsibility for clarifying requirements, providing estimates, scheduling work, and subsequently delivering the solution; but the Product Owner is *solely responsible* for the requirements-gathering, business clarification, and assignment of priorities. It is assumed that the Product Owner has separately collaborated with all the relevant business areas prior to the sprint planning session. It is equally assumed the Product Owner has sufficient business knowledge, vision, objectivity, and time to ensure the resulting requirements represent the best possible solution for the organization.

At the end of each iteration, a *sprint review* is undertaken, which includes a demonstration of work completed and confirmation of whether the developed software meets the needs of the business. Again, in this session, the Product Owner is generally expected to *individually represent* the cumulative interest of all affected business areas. There is opportunity for other business representatives to attend these sessions where needed, but the Product Owner is the primary representative who needs to assess and reconcile their feedback for the Agile development team.

As development work is undertaken during the sprint – and the high-level requirements that were discussed with the Product Owner are implemented in the working software –

the Agile team is likely to have questions regarding the exact behavior required in the solution, including the application of specific business rules, the clarification of supporting materials, and the viability of alternative approaches. Where the Product Owner is available to assist the developers during the iteration, there is opportunity to jointly address these questions through discussion, demonstration of software in progress, and/or requests for additional information to be gathered from the business areas. Where the Product Owner is *not available* to assist, however, these questions are often answered by the Agile development team to the best of their abilities, or deferred to the next Sprint Review, which could be several weeks away. In either case, the lack of direct access to the Product Owner means the team risks doing unnecessary work, or work that will need to be modified in subsequent iterations.

Although Agile methodologies are inherently designed to accommodate unexpected and uncontrollable change, they are equally designed to mitigate risk up front and to minimize wasted work during the development process. Expending development effort on capabilities that do not meet the needs of the business and will, therefore, need to be modified is not an encouraged outcome of these methodologies; it is the unintended result of not having the correct business resources available to the Agile team when they are needed.

This one example alone highlights the disparity between the rich collaborative opportunities that Agile methodologies provide to the development team, and the relatively little equivalent support provided for the business areas. To date, the scope of Agile methodologies has focused primarily on the work required to deliver relevant and successful *software solutions*; therefore, the focus has been on what is needed to support the Agile development team in their work. This approach may be ideal when the best solution for the business is a software product, and the business users are sufficiently knowledgeable and available to the team when they need input. In all other situations, however, it would be beneficial for the business users to get an equivalent opportunity for collaboration, that is, to be *paired* with resources who can work with them to:

- research and assess the business requirements,
- identify opportunities for resolving business issues outside of the software,
- assign business-value-driven priorities to the features, and
- communicate with the Agile developers throughout the project to clarify their business requirements.

Having a skilled business analyst on the Agile team provides business users with the opportunity to have *peer support* in the identification, valuation, clarification, testing, and rollout of their most critical business requirements. It also provides the Agile team members with a business-knowledgeable resource who is available to work *hands-on* with them throughout the project. All of this can substantially improve the relevance and business value of the delivered solution. So why is the Agile business analyst not already a part of every Agile team?

The disappearance of the traditional business analyst

One of the best ways to explain why most Agile development teams do not already have an Agile business analyst is by comparing a traditional waterfall IT project team to an Agile project team. The traditional project team is generally comprised of six distinctive roles:

- Developer
- Tester
- Systems architect
- Business analyst
- Technical writer
- Team leader.

Depending on the nature of the project, the traditional IT project team may also include the following roles:

- Data analyst
- Database specialist
- Network specialist
- Security specialist
- Trainer
- Quality and compliance specialist.

In most cases, the assignment of a person to a role on a traditional IT project team identifies the work that will be done exclusively by that resource. Developers code. Testers test. Never the twain shall meet. On smaller projects, traditional IT project team members may be asked to take on more than one of these roles, but that is usually out of necessity, not by design.

On multidisciplinary Agile project teams, these roles are deliberately blurred. Each member of the team has a primary skill set, but the roles they undertake throughout the project will vary, depending on the most immediate needs of the solution. In some cases, a required resource with specialty skills (e.g. security specialist, network specialist, quality and compliance specialist) is not a dedicated member of the Agile team, but is called upon when needed to provide their expertise.

Agile approaches do not negate the need for each of the 12 traditional IT project functions in a successful IT project; they assert that it is better for these roles to be shared among the Agile development team members than dedicated to individual resources. Having said that, there appears to be a bias toward a handful of these project functions as primary skill sets on Agile teams.

The typical Agile project team has a core set of resources who are skilled at coding. (In some cases, these may be the *only* resources dedicated to the team.) In addition to this core set of skilled coders, the Agile team ideally includes one or more software testers as dedicated team members, as their involvement encourages and confirms the delivery of high-quality outputs throughout the project.

If the required solution is particularly complex, the Agile team may also include a resource who has a primary skill set as a systems architect. Otherwise, the role of designing the solution is shared among the team members. Similarly, a project with significant database design or legacy data migration work may necessitate the assignment of experienced database design and data analysis specialists on the team. If not, these roles are also taken on by the development team, with input from specialists where needed.

As Agile teams are designed to be self-managing, there is rarely the need to include a dedicated team leader in the group. An Agile team may have senior team members who guide and advise the less experienced resources, but that tends to occur through team collaboration, and natural skills and strengths compensation, not because someone is officially nominated to lead the team.

Trainers may also work with the Agile team in preparation for pre- and post-implementation training, but they are generally not assigned as dedicated members of the team throughout the project. (One exception would be a project that regularly releases functionality to a live environment, where there is a corresponding need for the ongoing development of training materials and delivery of training to users.) It should also be noted that the active participation of business users throughout an Agile project can sometimes negate (or minimize) the need for extensive user training on the system. In this case, the only training required may be system walkthrough sessions with the Agile developers and the business users as part of the live release.

The need for a technical writer (or, more accurately, a *traditional* technical writer) on the Agile team is a debated topic in the Agile community. As Agile methodologies encourage the use of face-to-face communication – and the review of working software – instead of documentation wherever possible, the need for a technical writer to produce system documents throughout the project is minimized. Where needed, a skilled technical writer may be brought in to create an essential set of system documents at the end of the project timeline, particularly those documents required for post-implementation support, compliance, and audit purposes. There is usually, however, no need for reams of documentation to be produced in support of Agile development work as it is progressing. Similar to the model described for trainers, if an Agile project has minimal pre- and post-implementation documentation requirements, the team members may be able to produce most of the needed documentation themselves.

The role of the traditional business analyst on an Agile project team is, however, not as straightforward as the roles previously described. With technical writers and trainers, the timing of their involvement – and their outputs – may differ in an Agile project, but their function remains essentially the same as in traditional projects. Conversely, for business analysts to be valuable members of an Agile team, their role must shift from *traditional* business analysis to *Agile* business analysis.

The emergence of the *Agile* business analyst

If you ask anyone who has worked on a traditional IT project what the role of the business analyst is, they will most likely tell you they are responsible for analyzing user requirements and for writing the detailed functional specifications used for development work. The traditional business analyst is seen to be a key resource in the 'requirements phase' of the project, undertaking a range of analysis and documentation activities, including:

- requirements-gathering activities (stakeholder interviews, workshops, legacy system reviews)
- specification documentation, and
- specification sign-off.

All of these activities usually occur before development work is allowed to begin and, in some cases, may take several months to complete. On a traditional project, developers are generally put in a 'holding pattern' awaiting the delivery of signed-off specification documentation by the business analysts.

During the 'development phase' of the project, the traditional business analyst may also be involved in updating the specifications to include further detail to clarify technical or business-driven changes to the originally agreed requirements.

As traditional business analysts tend to have an intimate knowledge of the functional specifications, they can also be involved in the system testing, technical writing, and training activities at the end of a traditional IT project.

There are other roles the business analyst may serve in support of traditional IT projects (e.g. business case development, assistance in funding submissions) – and other work they may do independent of the software development (e.g. business process reengineering) – but the typical image of a traditional IT business analyst is the person who hands the development team piles of specification documentation, and then works with them to interpret what it all means.

In an Agile project, there is no need to create piles of upfront documentation, as the business users work directly with the Agile developers to identify and clarify their requirements, generally through face-to-face meetings and hands-on review of the software in progress. This creates a *direct line of communication* between the business users who know what they need, and the developers who know how to deliver their requirements in the most technically achievable way.

Equally, there is no need for a business analyst to clarify specifications as part of the development work. Any questions the developers have can be answered directly by the business user as part of their review sessions and, where appropriate, through ad hoc phone calls and e-mails.

On occasion, the Agile team may even get the benefit of having the business user *co-located* with the developers, which makes it even easier to call upon them with questions and clarifications while development work is underway.

With the development team having this degree of direct access to the business user to identify and clarify requirements, what possible value is there in having a business analyst as the middleman in the process? The truth is that when the role of the business analyst is constrained to the *traditional* IT business analyst as just described, that is, as the documenter and interpreter of piles of specifications, the answer is relatively little value. It is, therefore, no surprise that Agile teams may feel that having a dedicated business analyst is unnecessary for their projects.

This premise, however, is based upon a number of assumptions the Agile team has made about the participation of the business user in the process, specifically:

- The business user knows exactly what the solution needs to do to achieve the business objectives of the organization, and is able to clearly articulate these requirements to the developers.
- The business user knows the relative business value and priority of every requested feature.
- The business user is accurately representing the perspectives of all stakeholders in the solution.
- The business user is objective enough to see beyond their 'business as usual' activities.
- The business user has considered the full spectrum of options for addressing their business requirements *beyond* the software solution, including:
    - business process improvements
    - targeted staff training

    - restructuring of roles
    - policy updates, and
    - more effective corporate communication.
- The business user will continue to be available to the Agile team as needed throughout the project, including clarification of requirements, acceptance testing, training, user documentation, and post-implementation support.

In some cases, the Agile team is fortunate enough to have a business user who is sufficiently knowledgeable, objective, forward thinking, and available to effectively deliver all of these things. More often than not, however, the business user needs assistance in one or more of these areas.

One example is a business user who has extensive knowledge of the current environment and the legacy systems, but who has no direct experience in assessing the business value of proposed features; or one who has spoken with numerous stakeholders about what they want in the system, but has a bias toward the features they personally find valuable.

Another example is a business user who has a fixed image of how the system should behave and is not open to considering alternative options offered by the development team.

A third example is the rare business user who has extensive knowledge about the requirements, sufficient experience to valuate and prioritize each feature, and objectivity to see beyond their current work practices, but who is so good at their primary job that they have limited time to spend with the development team.

In all of these cases, it would benefit the Agile team – and the organization – to have a *dedicated Agile business analyst* available to work alongside the business user, helping them to:

- gather business requirements from the broad range of system stakeholders – and to identify the underlying business drivers for requested software features
- think beyond their current work environment, business processes, and systems to leverage the potential opportunities a new solution (or new features in an existing solution) can provide
- assess whether the identified requirements are best met by the software solution, by changes to business practices, or by a combination of both
- identify and quantify the relative business value of each requested feature in order to provide a value-driven priority list to the development team
- abstract the specific software features requested by stakeholders into more general business requirements (e.g. user stories) that can be interpreted by the development team to provide the best technical solution
- put together any additional information needed to support the requirements (e.g. sample reports, detailed business rules)
- represent the interests of the business user on those occasions when they have limited availability to work with the development team
- undertake more time-consuming activities on behalf of the business users, such as detailed acceptance testing or training

- establish and implement rollout strategies, including stakeholder communication, supporting documentation, and training materials for each target audience.

In some respects, the role of the Agile business analyst is similar to that of the traditional IT business analyst. Much of the preliminary work in gathering requirements, assessing the subset of requirements best addressed in a software solution, and prioritizing software features is the input that would traditionally go into the detailed specification documentation. The key difference with an *Agile* business analyst is that the gathered and prioritized requirements are conveyed to the development team in user stories and face-to-face communication, instead of reams of documentation (which can actually be a welcome change for the business analyst who dreads writing up these specification documents as much as developers dread receiving them!)

The availability of the business user throughout an Agile project also shifts the role of the Agile business analyst from representative to facilitator, which is another welcome change for the business analyst. Instead of spending time chasing down the business area for clarification and detail, the Agile business analyst equally benefits from getting real-time feedback from the business user. This allows the Agile business analyst to focus on working with the business user and the development team to establish an achievable set of software features that genuinely meet the needs of the business, not on trying to recall the details from a discussion with the business area three weeks ago.

Most importantly, however, the inclusion of an Agile business analyst on the Agile team means the business user has someone to *pair with*, giving the business user all of the knowledge sharing and quality control benefits that pairing provides to the Agile developers.

Everything described in this section until now has focused on the work the Agile business analyst does in support of the development of the solution, but there are equally valuable roles the Agile business analyst can provide beyond the software development, including:

- assisting in project management and quality management compliance work
- identifying and implementing business process improvements in conjunction with the delivered solution
- helping to write business cases for additional project funding, where needed.

It is important to remember that business users generally have primary operational roles that will likely have been put on hold (or reduced) in order for them to be available to work with the Agile team during the project timeline. Once the solution is implemented, these business users will most likely need to return to their primary roles on a full-time basis, which substantially limits their ability to provide the ongoing support needed to ensure the delivered solution is successfully integrated into business operations. Where a business user may have limited post-implementation availability, the primary role of the Agile business analyst can be expanded to deliver any ongoing support needed, including: implementing business process, procedure, and policy changes; training new users; creating additional user documentation; addressing cross-departmental impacts; communicating with stakeholders; providing skills training; and establishing an operational helpdesk.

In this respect, the inclusion of an Agile business analyst has benefits for the Agile team that go beyond the development and release of the software.

Isn't the Agile developer also the business analyst?

If you are an Agile developer reading this section, you may be questioning why an Agile business analyst would be needed at all. Agile developers already work directly with the business users to identify and clarify their requirements. Why not provide Agile developers with the equivalent skills to help the business user gather, assess, valuate, prioritize, and communicate their requirements (and assist with post-implementation work)?

In theory, it would be possible to train Agile developers to broaden their direct communication with the business user to include these activities – in the same way Agile developers can act as system testers, technical writers, and trainers where needed – but it would not be in the best interest of the project. The following section explains why.

Individual strengths in multidisciplinary teams

As described earlier in this section, an Agile team is a cross-disciplinary group of people with varying levels of experience and expertise. Although each team member generally has a primary skill set (e.g. coding, system architecture, testing), every member of the team is expected to undertake whatever work is needed most urgently to deliver the solution in the agreed timeframe. Developers need to take on testing, technical writing, even training tasks, if that is what the project requires. But needing to do something and having it be your *primary focus* – and *strength* – are two very different things.

An experienced software tester is not only skilled in the mechanics of writing test plans, detailing test cases, and executing tests; they *think* like a tester. In requirements analysis and estimation meetings, their minds are generally focused on what would be required to test – and to break – each proposed feature, as well as what is needed to establish the supporting test environment and prepare required test data. Many experienced testers will also consider the development, technical writing, and training implications of the feature as part of their assessment, but their primary focus will generally be on the testing requirements.

In the spirit of test-driven development (TDD)[1], the members of the Agile team who are tasked to code requested features are also likely to be considering the testing implications in their requirements analysis (although generally their focus is more on unit testing than system testing). At the heart of their thinking, however, is how is this feature going to be built in the system, what other parts of the system may be impacted, and whether architectural design, database, or infrastructure changes are needed. The coders may undertake testing as part of their work, but their point of reference is usually from a development standpoint.

Similarly, an experienced technical writer initially assesses a solution based on what would be required to document system behavior, create context-sensitive help, and build

---

1 Test-driven development is an Agile practice that encourages software developers to create the tests that will be used to validate the code they are building prior to undertaking development work. See *www.codeproject.com/articles/47747/test-driven-development-tdd-step-by-step-part-1-in* for further detail.

other necessary system documentation. It is not that technical writers cannot consider the development, testing, or training implications of each proposed feature; it is just not where their mind naturally focuses. It is the difference between writing a document the project requires and *being* a technical writer.

An experienced Agile business analyst comes to the table with an inherent and instinctive focus on understanding how the business operates and where the system fits within these operations. They view software as an enabler to a bigger business objective, not the complete solution. Although some business analysts have detailed technical knowledge, they are usually not the ones who designed the system architecture or built the software. This gives them the objectivity to view the system with an awareness of – but not a primary focus on – technical constraints (with a reliance on the developers to advise on the most technically achievable solution). Equally, Agile business analysts work with the business areas, but are generally not one of the hands-on business users. This allows them to *objectively* assess the needs of the business without being too close to existing procedures and legacy systems to see beyond them.

Including an Agile business analyst gives the Agile development team an experienced liaison whose primary focus is to deliver a *complete solution* to the business, which includes:

- delivered software
- supporting documentation and system training
- corresponding changes to business procedures, processes, and policies
- identification of skills shortages and required skills training for the business areas

- assistance in identifying and addressing potential impacts on other departments
- support for future funding submissions to address known gaps in the solution, where needed.

In some cases, the Agile business analyst may also be able to *pre-emptively* address issues by working with the business user prior to discussions with the Agile development team, ensuring their requested features are truly necessary and prioritized by the *business value* they can deliver.

This does not mean Agile developers cannot, or do not, undertake some degree of business analysis as part of their role. I have worked with some incredibly insightful developers who couple their technical expertise with a big picture perspective on the business implications of requested features. They are able to step away from the solution itself to consider the business drivers and the potential impacts on ongoing business processes in the organization. They genuinely understand the delivered software is only part of the bigger business solution. I have equally worked with developers who are completely focused on the technical impacts of each feature. When they do question a requested feature, it is generally to clarify exactly how it should appear or behave in the system. It never strikes them to stop and question *why* the feature is being requested altogether. Most Agile developers fall somewhere in between this spectrum. The question, however, is not whether the Agile developer is sufficiently skilled to take on this role. The question is whether it is fair to ask them to do it in the first place.

For someone whose primary strength – and time commitment – is coding, is it reasonable to ask that person to equally serve as tester, technical writer, system architect, trainer, and business analyst on the team? Like any good cross-disciplinary team, there needs to be a balance between what team members are capable of doing and how work should reasonably be distributed among the team members. Agile team members are expected to think holistically and consider other perspectives in their work; however, asking Agile developers to actively take on five or more concurrent roles throughout the project is doing a disservice to the team member, the team, and the project.

There is another, perhaps more delicate reason why Agile developers are not in the best position to serve as the business analysts on the team: the business user is likely to see Agile developers as being too close to the solution to offer wholly objective, business-driven advice. This may be an incorrect assumption (or an over-generalization) on their part, but it is a genuine concern. This means that, when an Agile developer is trying to persuade a business user to consider an alternative solution to the feature the business area had envisaged, the business user may have some scepticism about their motives. (Are they offering the best solution for my area, or the easiest one for them to implement?) This scepticism may be wholly unfounded, and completely undeserved, but it can still be a lingering question in the mind of the business user that could make them more resistant to compromise. (Not unlike you questioning the objectivity of the advice the mechanic gives about fixing your car. The mechanic is both the expert and the one who stands to gain the most financially from leading you in a particular direction.) The business user may also have doubts about whether the Agile developer is in a position to truly understand the needs of the business.

Again, this might be an unfair characterization, but it can be an impediment to negotiation on features.

On the contrary, the Agile business analyst is generally not seen by the business user as having a vested interest in technical decisions. If anything, the business user sees the Agile business analyst as an impartial facilitator with a reasonable understanding of both the business requirements and the software solution to offer fair advice. This means Agile developers may be able to leverage the involvement of the Agile business analyst to persuade the business user where needed in a far more effective way than trying to convince them on their own, particularly when discussing (and negotiating) the business requirements.

It is fair to say that most requirements discussions and in-progress software reviews do not involve significant back-and-forth negotiation between the business users and the Agile developers. There may be times when the expectations of the business users do not align directly with the proposed – or the developed – software, but these can usually be resolved on the spot. On the rare occasion an insurmountable mismatch of expectations does arise, however, it is really valuable to have an Agile business analyst in the process to allay concerns and facilitate a compromise that satisfies the needs of all project team members.

Another reason for expanding the team to include an Agile business analyst *in conjunction with* the Agile developers is to support the range of other functions external to the software development (e.g. business process improvements, stakeholder communication, assistance in future funding requests), which do not have a current equivalent on the Agile team. For most Agile approaches, developers rely on the business users to undertake these activities, or to enlist the appropriate resources to do this work. Although these activities are technically independent of the software development, they are intrinsically tied to the ongoing success of the delivered solution and, therefore, the perceived success of the Agile project by the organization. The closer that Agile business analysts are to Agile teams and the developed solutions, the better positioned they will be to communicate accurately with target audiences about the solution, to implement corresponding business processes, and to 'sell' the solution to senior management if ongoing funding is needed. This role is particularly important in situations where the business user is not available to undertake these tasks.

All of this means that the Agile business analyst has critical skills that *complement* the other members of the Agile development team. The Agile business analyst equally plays a role in the business area, both in pairing with the business user and in assisting in the integration of the delivered solution into ongoing business activities. In effect, the Agile business analyst is a working member of both the business area and the Agile development team. When it comes to staffing and funding, however, the Agile business analyst most likely needs to be officially tied to one of these groups. The real question is which group should the Agile business analyst belong to?

Where does the Agile business analyst belong?

There is an argument to say that the functions the Agile business analyst performs are primarily the responsibility of the business users. Agile methodologies tend to assume the business users undertake all of the preliminary work that goes into identifying, valuating, and prioritizing the business requirements presented to the Agile development team, as well as any work required to integrate the delivered solution into the operations of the business area. The Agile development team is responsible for developing and delivering the solution, but the business users take ownership of ensuring the requested functionality and the delivered solution meets their needs.

Based on this assumption, why not leave it with the business users to hire the Agile business analyst for their own work, independent of the Agile team? Similarly, why not require any resource who supports the business users (e.g. trainers, technical writers) to be staffed by the business area? The answer lies in the delivered solution.

Having the Agile business analyst as a core part of the Agile team enables them to understand the solution in far greater detail. It promotes more frequent communication of business requirements and system functionality throughout the development process. Most important, it allows the Agile development team to leverage the Agile business analyst as a key resource to assist in any work the team needs, including analyzing the data mapping, cleansing, and migration requirements; identifying system security, performance, and capacity requirements; specifying external system integration business rules and constraints; confirming desired system behavior with the business users and other stakeholders during the development process; testing; documentation; and training. As a core part of the Agile team, Agile business analysts are best positioned to assist developers in their mission to increase the quality, flexibility, and relevance of the delivered solution.

Truth be told, it is good to have a business analyst be part of the project team in any capacity, even if they are effectively a representative of the business users. It is more valuable, however, when the Agile business analyst is positioned to work as closely with the developers as possible, as the software they build is the heart of the business solution. Having the Agile business analyst as a core member of the Agile team provides that opportunity.

At the end of the day, it does not matter whether solution-related activities are officially positioned as an extension of the Agile development team or as a function of the business users. It is the responsibility of the shared project team, the Agile developers and the business area combined, to ensure a successful solution is delivered to the organization. The Agile business analyst can provide a valuable and vital role in either capacity.

CHAPTER 4: WHAT ARE THE RISKS OF NOT HAVING AN AGILE BUSINESS ANALYST?

The limitations of requirements review sessions

As described in the previous section, Agile approaches generally task the business users with gathering, documenting, and prioritizing the business requirements of the system; and the Agile development team with clarifying the intended system behavior, identifying possible alternative options in the solution, and estimating the amount of work required to deliver agreed features. The business requirements of the system are usually prepared and prioritized by the business users *prior to* the requirements review sessions with the Agile development team. It is expected that the business users have consulted with the necessary stakeholders, identified the core set of functionality the solution needs to provide, and assigned priorities based on the relative business value of each feature. It is also expected that the business users have considered the operational implications of the requested functionality before these sessions, including whether or not there are viable alternatives to addressing the business requirement *outside of* the software solution. The prioritized list of features the business user brings to the requirements review sessions is, therefore, intended to be assessed by the Agile development team primarily for technical feasibility, not questioned for relevance to the business altogether.

There is limited opportunity for the Agile development team to know how much – or how little – validation of the prioritized list of requirements has occurred prior to the requirements review session. As discussed, current Agile methodologies do not include a formal *pairing model* for the business user to provide validation, knowledge-sharing, and quality control of the business requirements, in the same way the pairing of Agile team members provides these controls in the software development process throughout the project. This begs the question of how, if at all, an *objective* review of the stated business requirements was undertaken by anyone other than the business user in the preparation process prior to the requirements review session. Did anyone take a critical look at each feature to consider alternatives to delivering the stated capability as part of the software solution? Did someone outside of the business area provide a sanity check to ensure the requested feature is not a throwback to legacy system behavior or extraneous to ongoing business operations? Did the business users take a broader look at the business processes (and policies) that may be driving the perceived need for a system capability to see if these should be changed instead of the software? In many cases, the requirements review session with the Agile development team is the first time anyone other than the business users has undertaken a detailed review of the requirements, but this may not be the right forum (or audience) for identifying business alternatives to requested solution capabilities.

In the requirements review sessions, the primary focus of the Agile development team is to get sufficient information about each requested system feature to:

- understand the *intended behavior* of the feature (screen design, business rules, dependencies, constraints),
- determine the technical feasibility of the feature, and

- estimate the amount of work required to deliver that feature in the solution.

Where a requested feature is reasonably simple to deliver, it is rare the Agile development team would question the *business drivers* behind the feature, that is, whether it should be included in the solution altogether. The Agile development team is working from the assumption that the business user has undertaken the necessary background work to confirm the business value and priority of every feature requested before the requirements review session. That is, unless the requested feature is beyond the capabilities of the solution.

When the Agile development team sees a requested feature as more complex, or too difficult to deliver in the current system architecture, they may be less willing to accept the stated requirement on face value. In this circumstance, the Agile developers may probe the underlying need for the feature with the business user in order to look for more viable technical alternatives. (The underlying motive of the developers may also be to have the complex feature moved down the priority list or removed from the list altogether!)

In questioning a feature, the Agile development team is generally not in a position to look beyond the solution to consider business process changes that could sufficiently address the requirement in lieu of the software. The developers are also rarely in a position to persuade the business user to reconsider the requirement, as they would generally not be familiar enough with the business operations to counter any argument made by the business user in support of the feature.

4: What are the Risks of Not Having an Agile Business Analyst?

The bottom line is that there is no clear process in Agile approaches for ensuring requested business capabilities are best addressed through features in the software solution, and not through business process changes, policy reviews, re-skilling of staff, etc. There is equally no clear process for ensuring each requested feature is given an equivalent level of scrutiny by the Agile development team. If the feature at the top of the priority list is a simple change to an existing report format, the team will generally jump straight into the estimation discussion. On the other hand, if the feature at the top of the list is a three-dimensional graphical rendering of an existing report, the team is likely to ask further questions to see where the requirement can be simplified. The truth, however, is that it is not the technical complexity of the requested feature that should be the determining factor in whether or not the Agile team questions the value of a requirement. The ideal Agile approach should include practices that confirm the business value of requested features – and the best approach to addressing the requirement – before, during, and after these review sessions. This is one of the significant values an Agile business analyst can provide to the project.

The following example is taken from a project I worked on recently, where the business users proposed 12 updates to their commercial financial management system. The Agile development team was confident that 10 of the proposed updates were achievable, but had concerns about their ability to deliver two of the key features identified as high priority by the business users, specifically:

- Automatic reimbursement of travel expenses using a complex set of algorithms that combine duration of travel, point of origin, destination, and employee level, with over 400 potential combinations.

- Trend analysis of departmental budget utilization to provide a graphical year-by-year comparison of quarterly results.

These capabilities did not exist in the system, and the Agile developers were concerned they would be too complicated to build into the current architecture. The developers had investigated third-party products that may have been able to provide these capabilities, but they found the interfaces needed to provide the relevant data would also require significant development work.

The Agile development team knew the requested capabilities were not realistic to be delivered on their software platform within the project timeline. The business users were, however, insistent the software must provide these capabilities to address a substantial gap in their current management and reporting. Every alternative (and more achievable) technical option offered by the development team was seen by the business user as a compromise that was insufficient to meet their needs.

This scenario is an ideal situation for an Agile business analyst to facilitate the process by working with the business users on options that can address their requirements in ways that do not rely solely on software capabilities. For example:

Automatic reimbursement of travel expenses:

The Agile business analyst was able to work with the business users to identify the real business drivers behind this feature. In these discussions, it was identified that:

- The legacy process of having travelers manually enter their total expenses required the finance department to recalculate and reconcile each expense report by hand. This was extremely time-consuming and subject to human error. It also required follow-up discussions with the traveler where the total expenses submitted did not match the calculations done by finance.
- The business users had not yet analyzed their historical travel data to determine if there were any significant trends or commonalities in travel behavior. Knowing the business users were pressed for time, the Agile business analyst offered to assist the business users in gathering and assessing this data.

The analysis of the travel data undertaken by the Agile business analyst resulted in the following findings:

- Most of the travel undertaken (82 percent) is to one of four destinations.
- More than 75 percent of the travel is undertaken by non-executive staff.
- There are only two instances where a staff member needed to stay more than five business days, that is, over a weekend.

Based on this analysis, it was determined that only 13 of the 400 potential combinations of travel parameters are commonly used. This provided an opportunity for the development team to create *preset calculations* in the system for the most common combinations, with a *manual entry option* for providing totals where there are exception cases. The finance department still needed to reconcile these exceptions by hand, but the alternative approach proposed by the Agile business analyst had the potential to result in a 90 percent reduction in their current workload.

The alternative approach also resulted in a much less complicated technical solution that could be realistically built within the existing architecture, and which required substantially less testing than the 400 potential combinations. This meant that the objective identified by the business users was able to be delivered with achievable system features and minimal compromise.

Graphical trend analysis of departmental budget utilization:

In discussion with the business users, the Agile business analyst identified the real driver behind this feature was the need to more clearly identify when a department had exceeded or under-spent their quarterly budget allocation by more than 10 percent, and to determine whether this was a common occurrence or an exception case. The finance department wanted the opportunity to intervene if quarterly results were indicating a potential budget blowout for the financial year.

To address this requirement, the Agile business analyst worked with the business users on viable alternatives that would achieve their objectives without requiring a complex technical solution, such as:

- clearly flagging budget variations of 10 percent or more in the current quarterly report
- allowing the finance department to view historical reporting data for any section flagged as significantly over- or under-spending
- providing an export feature for historical data that can be imported into a spreadsheet if further analysis is required.

In addition, the Agile business analyst worked with the business users on instituting changes to organizational reporting procedures, including requiring section heads to actively notify the finance department if their budget utilization falls outside of identified thresholds during the quarter. This allowed finance to proactively work with the section to resolve the issue *before* each reporting cycle was complete – and reduced the dependency on the software to resolve the issue.

Providing these alternative solution options, along with corresponding changes in reporting procedures, allowed the Agile development team to address the most critical business drivers without building unnecessary 'bells and whistles' into the system. In this case, the alternative solution also introduced a proactive reporting option outside of the system, which may be more effective than the retrospective identification of issues within the system. Equally important, the Agile business analyst helped the business users to distinguish between the feature they had visualized as the required solution (i.e. graphical trend reports) and the underlying business drivers that could be addressed more realistically and cost-effectively with a simpler technical solution.

Without the involvement of the Agile business analyst, the Agile development team may have had to reluctantly agree to build the original complex functionality requested by the business users (even if doing this meant compromising other high priority features). Alternatively, the business users may have had to agree to *not include* this feature due to the technical complexity, which would have meant the delivered solution was unable to successfully address some of their business issues.

In this example, it was the *technical complexity* of two of the requested features that initiated a critical review of the business value of each feature and whether viable alternative options were available. In reality, the same level of scrutiny should be applied to *every* requested feature in the solution, ideally even before the requirements review session is begun, but this can have minimal value if the business users are trying to achieve this on their own.

There is an inherent risk in having unsupported business users tasked with the sole responsibility of putting together the business requirements for a solution. Are they too close to their current work practices to see beyond them? Have they consulted with every user group who will be impacted by the solution? Is their prioritization of features based on their personal preferences (even unintentionally), instead of being based on an *objective* assessment of the capabilities that will deliver the greatest value to the organization overall?

There is an equivalent risk when the unsupported business users intimately understand their own work area, but are not fully aware of the overarching policy or regulatory constraints that can impact their business decisions (let alone the integration, data, or security implications of their requested capabilities).

The truth is that many business users are so familiar with the current operations that they struggle to see beyond them. The new system features they are requesting may, in fact, be artifacts of their legacy procedures, not the best use of the available technology. Pairing an Agile business analyst with the business user *before* the requirements review session provides an opportunity for objective review and confirmation of requested software features *in advance of* presenting these features to the Agile development team.

Software is only part of the solution

To date, the scope of Agile methodologies has focused primarily on the work required to deliver relevant and successful *software solutions*. There is, however, substantial opportunity for these approaches to add value beyond the delivery of software, which may not always be evident, even when business users are paired directly with the Agile developers.

The Agile model of pairing developers directly with business users has several strengths:

- Developers get firsthand knowledge of business user needs.
- Requirements are conveyed in face-to-face discussions with the business user, not through piles of documentation.
- Developers can ask questions about – and get real-time feedback on – specific capabilities.
- The software under development can be used as a tool to facilitate communication and clarify requirements.

This direct interaction is a decidedly more effective way for the Agile development team to understand and confirm business needs than traditional waterfall approaches, which often separated the technical team from the subject matter experts during the development phase. By working together directly, business users are able to influence the solution in a much more tangible and satisfying way, and Agile developers no longer need to interpret system requirements from distilled, two-dimensional specification documents.

In fact, this approach is so effective the participants rarely question what could be *missing from these discussions.*

Each of the participants comes into the discussion with a definitive area of expertise: the business user provides an intimate understanding of their area of the organization, including their objectives, their current processes, and any impediments to achieving their goals. If there is an existing system in place, the business user can also offer insights into what does – and does not – work well in the current solution. Equally, the Agile developer brings specialist knowledge of technical capabilities, limitations, and achievable outcomes to guide the business user toward a more realistic system. Combined, the participants are in a position to provide a strong foundation for identifying the best software solution to meet the ongoing needs of the business. What they may lack, however, is the ability to see the solution *beyond* the software, such as business process improvements, policy changes, greater cross-departmental communication, skills training, adjustments to management reporting structures, or changes to corporate frameworks.

Asking business users to clarify and prioritize their requested features focuses the discussion on *refining the software*, not on challenging the business value of their requested functionality, or considering options for addressing business issues that do not involve the software. Not having this broader discussion, however, can substantially impact the value of the delivered solution. The following section explains why.

The danger of the unquestioned business user

Direct engagement between the Agile team and the business users

When business users are presented with the opportunity to create a new system – or to replace an existing one – there is a tendency for them to see the solution as their one great chance to make their work easier, to improve efficiency, to correct all of the previous wrongs that have historically impacted their business area. This opportunity can create a strong sense of enthusiasm for the project among the business users, as well as excitement for all of the potential that a new solution can provide. In some respects, their eagerness to identify the capabilities of the new solution is a very positive thing, as this means the business users are likely to put in enormous amounts of effort in support of the project. There is, however, an equivalent risk of the business users reverting to a 'kid in a candy shop' mentality, making the specifications for the proposed system an unfettered *wish list* of everything they could possibly imagine.

Agile approaches endeavor to address the potential of business users coming to the table with an 'all and sundry' capabilities list by requiring them to assign priorities to all of the requested features. The intention of this approach is not to unduly restrict the business users from considering the full scope of solution capabilities; it is intended to force the business users to think critically about the capabilities they are requesting, and to identify which of these capabilities will provide the organization with the greatest business value. The resulting list of prioritized features is what drives the decision of what the Agile development team will focus on in each iteration, and shapes the scope of high-priority capabilities the solution overall will deliver. When business users are left to make these priority decisions on their own, however, the outcomes may not reflect what the business truly needs in the solution.

As one example, consider a situation where the business users have requested the Agile development team build an online application form that will allow organizations to nominate themselves for an industry award. The business users detail the requested features of the online form, such as:

- the 55 information fields applicants need to fill in, including the preferred order and layout of the fields
- the subset of 32 fields that are mandatory
- the business rules for the calculation fields
- the selection values for the drop-down lists
- the help text that should appear on the screen, next to each field
- the instructions and due dates for the organizations to send their application fee checks through the mail.

In the requirements review session, the requested form capability is described by the business users in a few high-level user stories, for example:

As an award applicant, I want to be able to submit my application form online so I can fill it in more easily and be sure all of the information is correctly provided.

As an award application processor, I want the information submitted in the application forms to be complete and accurate so I can easily add them to the application processing system.

As an award application processor, I want the system to automatically calculate the required application payment amount so I do not need to spend extra time contacting the applicant if the amount of the check they send to us is incorrect.

These user stories are accompanied by copies of the paper forms the applicants are currently using, with some penciled-in notes from the business users on the fields that need to be added, updated, or removed.

The requirements review session between the business users and the Agile team is likely to center around the details of implementing the requested form, with clarification questions from the developers, such as:

- Can the fields have a different layout for the online screen than on the paper form?
- Should all 55 fields appear on one screen, or be broken down into multiple screens?
- If the fields are broken down into multiple screens, does the applicant need to have filled in all of the mandatory fields on a screen before they can progress to the next one?
- Can the help text be presented to the applicant when they hover over a field (or in a pop-up window) instead of being displayed on the form itself?

The discussion with the business users may even extend to the Agile development team suggesting system capabilities the business users may not have considered, such as:

- offering *online payments* as an alternative option to receiving application fee checks through standard mail (as the business users may have been so used to processing payments by check, they may not have even considered the online platform could offer them a more efficient alternative)

- integrating the application form directly into the application processing system, in order to avoid staff re-keying of the application form details.

Both of these suggestions from the Agile development team would provide efficiencies the business users may not have considered on their own. Each of them does, however, also require further investigation by the Agile development team to confirm:

- What online payment services are available, and how much work is involved in integrating with these services?
- What system interfaces are available for the application processing system, and what are the data structures for the stored information in the system?

The investigation required for these external systems is one of the areas where an Agile business analyst could help the Agile developers, including ascertaining the required data mappings and business rules for the application processing system. Having the Agile business analyst do this research would free the developers to focus on building the online form screens and validation logic.

From a technology standpoint, the Agile developers are likely to feel the requested online application form is achievable, with the knowledge that the outcome of the investigation into external systems may impact the team's ability to include these additional features. Based on this, the Agile development team would most likely agree to proceed with the work as requested for the next four weeks, with the aim of presenting the online application form to the business users for their approval at the next iteration review session.

From a *business-value* standpoint, however, the decision to go ahead with the online application form may not be quite as straightforward.

The value of including an Agile business analyst

If the business users had been given an opportunity to pair with an Agile business analyst prior to the requirements review session, the Agile business analyst would have been in a position to question key business elements of the requested online form with the business users before the meeting with the Agile development team, including:

- Are all 55 of the information fields required to process the application form? What about the 32 mandatory fields? Can the form details be streamlined?
- What is the actual business process for assessing each application? Are there information fields needed that are not currently on the form?
- Is there supporting information that applicants need to provide during the assessment process, for example, copies of their annual report, balance sheets? Can any of these details be provided as attachments with the application form?
- Should applicants be able to save draft forms and return to them later? (In which case, there would be a number of technical implications to discuss with the Agile development team for saving temporary form details, creating and authenticating user accounts, removing draft forms after a specified period of time, etc.)
- Are there any policy or regulatory mandates that govern the application process?

- How many applications are received in the eligibility period on average? Of the applications received, what portion proceeds to undergoing a full assessment? What does the application review team do with application forms that are invalid or insufficient?
- How much does it cost the organization to process each paper-based application?
- Who receives the checks mailed in by the applicants? How is the check amount reconciled against the application form?

The outcome of these questions may simply have been a confirmation of the business users' originally requested online application form capability with, perhaps, a bit more insight into the overhead costs for processing the paper-based forms, and the net gains the online application process can provide for the organization. Conversely, the outcome of these questions may have revealed information that substantially impacts the business value of developing the online application form, including:

- Of the 2,200 applications received each year, only 390 applications are from eligible organizations. This means including an information page with the paper application form that explains the application criteria more clearly could reduce the number of applications received by 60 percent, which could substantially decrease the overhead costs of processing the applications.
- 21 of the 55 information fields are only used in the application assessment process where the applicant has an exceptional circumstance. These fields are unnecessary for most applicants.

- The regulations that govern the industry award require that all applications are submitted with the signature of the chief executive officer and an original imprint of the company seal. There is no accommodation for e-signatures or scanned copies of the company seal.

The first piece of this additional information impacts the net gain the organization will receive from building the online application form. Instead of saving on the cost of processing more than 2,000 applications per annum, the organization would only be saving the cost of processing 400 applications. Is the overhead cost of building the online application form worth the net savings?

The second piece of this additional information impacts how much work is involved for the applicants who complete the form, and the staff members on the application review team, as well as the number of fields that need to be stored and mapped in the system. Too often, unquestioned business users will assume an online form should be the equivalent of the paper form with some data entry and validation efficiencies. Further analysis with the assistance of the Agile business analyst may, however, reveal there are fields on the original form that are rarely (or never) used, or which were required to support outdated business processes. Reducing the number of fields on the form to only those required in the current process can substantially reduce the operational overheads of processing the form, as well as the development cost. It can also make the process less onerous for the applicants.

Both of these are important efficiencies that could have been gained by involving the Agile business analyst in the initial discussions with the business users – but the third bullet point is, by far, the most critical. If the analysis that had been done by the Agile business analyst – or by the business users in response to the questions asked by the Agile business analyst – revealed it would be impossible to process the application form without the *written signature* of the chief executive officer and *an original imprint* of the company seal being mailed to the organization, there may actually be *little to no business value* in building the online form at all. Even if the form fields could be submitted online, the applicant would still need to mail in these additional details, and the application processing team would still need to process the form manually.

This is not to say that every time an Agile business analyst pairs with the business users prior to meeting with the Agile development team, the result of the analysis will be a showstopper, or even a significant issue. It is, however, likely these discussions will identify operational efficiencies and other benefits that can be gained by objectively reviewing the business drivers and business processes around each requested capability. These efficiencies can reduce the amount of wasted work done by the Agile development team and increase the overall business value of the delivered solution.

The tyranny of proximity

One of the primary reasons why it is valuable to have the Agile business analyst work with the business users to question their requested capabilities is it can be difficult for business users to be *truly objective* in their decision making. The business knowledge and expertise that makes a business user the best representative to work with the Agile development team may also unintentionally cloud their judgment. Where business users are too close to the current business processes to see beyond them, the Agile business analyst is able to provide an objective perspective on the most effective solution.

The online application form described in the previous section is an example of a situation where business users assumed that putting the current paper-based forms online would make the process more efficient. Without a peer resource to pair with them and question this assumption, it is likely this would have been the requested capability brought to the Agile development team in the requirements review session; and equally likely the online form – with online payments and integration into the application processing system – would have been the delivered solution. This means the Agile approach would have delivered a fully functional, high quality, business user-approved online application form that provided minimal net gains for the organization. In essence, the software development would have been a success, and the overall project would have been a failure.

What to do when the business user is not available

There will come a time in every Agile project when even the most well-intentioned business users will be unavailable to provide the Agile developers with real-time answers to their questions or with feedback on the software in progress. So what does the Agile development team do when the business users have limited (or no) availability to work with the developers?

Unless business users are assigned to work with the Agile team on a full-time basis, they will inevitably need to balance their ongoing involvement on the project with their day-to-day responsibilities. Iterative Agile methods (such as

Scrum) endeavor to mitigate this risk by ensuring the business users are *minimally* available to work with the team at the iteration planning and review sessions, that is, once every two to four weeks, but is this really enough involvement to address the risk of misaligned requirements and wasted development work? What happens if the Agile team needs information, decisions, or feedback from the business users to support *their* day-to-day work in the 10 to 20 working days in between these sessions?

Earlier in this section, it was identified that the enthusiasm of the business users for the potential of a new solution can be a double-edged sword. On the one hand, their excitement can motivate them to become incredibly involved in the project, freeing up their schedules to make themselves as available as possible to work with the Agile team. On the other hand, their excitement can also result in their going a bit overboard in specifying the capabilities of the new solution. This is why Agile approaches rely on the prioritization of features as the sanity check that keeps the business users' expectations grounded.

What was not identified is that the business users' initial excitement for the project is likely to be toned down over time, partially because of the novelty wearing off, but mostly because of the competing commitments of their primary roles.

Although the ongoing delivery of fully functional software that is the hallmark of Agile approaches is able to maintain levels of business user motivation far more than the 'wait and see' model of traditional waterfall approaches, the reality is that business users continue to have responsibilities in their day-to-day work that can place significant demands on their time – and on their focus. The working software that is presented at Agile iteration review sessions can re-ignite the enthusiasm of the business users, at least for a period of time. Eventually, however, the pressures of their daily operational commitments are likely to impact their availability. Even with the best of intentions, the business users may not always be as available to work with the Agile team as they would like. They are also human beings with personal commitments, sick days, and vacation time, all of which means they cannot be expected to be an ever-present resource on the project.

Generally, business users are required to commit themselves to be available at specific points in an Agile project timeline, particularly in the planning and review sessions. This means the Agile team will have the benefit of their focus and their input for at least one identified period in each iteration, but it does not guarantee they will be available throughout the development timeframe to provide additional detail, to answer questions, or to confirm capabilities. This may not appear to be a showstopper for the Agile team members, who are often happy to make preliminary design and functional decisions on behalf of the business users, knowing there is an imminent opportunity to confirm their assumptions in the next review session. It does, however, add a risk that the team will waste some time in building capabilities based on their *interpretation* of the requirements; not as much time as would be wasted in a traditional waterfall project, but it is time that could be focused on delivering more valuable outputs.

When the Agile team has a number of unanswered questions on the capabilities under development, the compounded time they spend working from incorrect assumptions can amount to several weeks of development resource effort that could be better utilized if the Agile developers were in a position to get real-time confirmation and feedback from the business areas *throughout* the iteration. This is one of the *avoidable risks* an Agile business analyst can help the Agile team to address.

Although Agile business analysts cannot provide the definitive answers that co-located business users could, they *are* able to:

- provide objective feedback on system capabilities on behalf of the business users
- investigate answers to outstanding questions with the relevant stakeholders
- collect and confirm business criteria (e.g. validation rules)
- gather and assess information from legacy systems, including system behavior, field structures, value lists, and data records.

The involvement of the Agile business analyst does not completely eliminate the risk of incorrect decisions being made when the business users are not available, but it can substantially minimize this risk and allow the Agile development team to more confidently progress their work.

The interesting thing is that, even when business users *are* available to provide input to the Agile developers, they may not have sufficient time (or skills) to do all of the research the team requires to get answers to their questions. For example, the business users may be able to advise the team on a requested operational report, including field names, field order, summary calculations, and page layouts. The business users may not, however, be in a position to advise the developers on where the data needed to populate the fields is stored, what business rules and restrictions need to be applied to the calculations, or how to handle records with invalid or missing data. When detailed questions like these arise in the development work, the business user will often need to investigate the requirement further before they are in a position to provide the developers with the answers they need. For business users who are pressed for time (or who do not have the technical knowledge to respond to these questions), the Agile business analyst can undertake the necessary investigation on behalf of the business area, and confirm the outcome of this research with them before presenting the results to the Agile developers for further action.

Similarly, the business users may not have the time to undertake any acceptance testing of the software in progress, other than in the designated testing timeframes (i.e. at the end of each iteration and/or prior to a scheduled release). Where this is the case, the Agile business analyst can undertake *preliminary acceptance testing* on the business users' behalf, providing them with initial results for their review, which allows them to provide the Agile developers with targeted feedback without taking up substantial amounts of the business users' limited time. The involvement of the Agile business analyst in the preliminary acceptance testing does not negate the need for the business users to undertake proper acceptance testing at the designated points in the project timeline. It does, however, reduce the potential for significant issues to arise at the end of an iteration (or, worse still, prior to a scheduled release). Anything the Agile business analyst can do to help the team to confirm capabilities earlier in the development cycle is one less issue (and risk) the team needs to resolve further down the track.

It is worthwhile noting that the Agile business analyst is also likely to establish a test structure and test cases in support of the preliminary acceptance testing work they do on behalf of the business users. These materials can then be used by the business users, at their discretion, when they are in a position to conduct their own acceptance testing, which can result in substantial time savings for them (and give them time to do more thorough hands-on testing).

Some Agile developers who are reading this book may not see the need for preliminary acceptance testing as a particularly urgent one. In their minds, the business users have numerous opportunities to see the working software throughout the project timeline, for example, in the review sessions at the end of each iteration. Accordingly, these Agile developers would argue the acceptance testing the business users undertake should not result in significant changes, as they will have already seen – and confirmed – the behavior and design of the developed software. The issue is that system walkthroughs do not provide the same opportunity for the business users to experience – and confirm – the solution as hands-on acceptance testing does.

As valuable as review sessions are in walking the business users through the working features of the developed solution, they are no substitute for the business users having the opportunity to work *hands-on* with the software over a period of time – or on an integrated platform that more closely reflects the live environment. This is the difference between seeing the functionality of a solution in a development environment, and undertaking acceptance testing of the solution in an integration environment with the full set of data populated, user permissions configured, and more realistic network performance. The acceptance testing work the business users undertake will, ideally, be done in an environment that is as close as possible to the live environment. This means performance and usability issues that may not have been apparent when there were 1,000 records in the database may become insurmountable when there are 100,000, one million or ten million records in the system. Although the Agile business analyst cannot pre-empt the availability of full data sets from the live environment before the Agile developers are in a position to do the complete migration, the Agile business analyst *can* work with the testers to populate higher volumes of data in the test environment to deliberately push the boundaries of the software interface and performance. This minimizes the likelihood of surprises further down the track when the business users are available to undertake the acceptance testing themselves.

Although iteration review sessions can provide an opportunity for the business users to give their initial feedback on the software presented, it is their *detailed hands-on review* of the software and their more comprehensive acceptance testing activities that will definitively confirm (or deny) the ability of the developed software to meet their ongoing business needs. The results of the business users' acceptance testing may not dramatically change the layout or the behavior of the system, but the functional or data issues they do find may not always be something that can be addressed by the Agile developers in the next iteration, or in time for the next scheduled release. This is one of the primary drivers for having the Agile business analyst assist in the acceptance testing work sooner in the project timeline – and more frequently – than the business users may be available to undertake this work.

Opportunities that could be missed

The Agile business analyst is able to undertake a number of other project activities on behalf of the business users when they have limited availability, including creating supporting documentation, preparing training materials, preparing (and assigning business values to) user stories for upcoming planning sessions, gathering supporting detail for user stories (e.g. sample reports), researching mandates and corporate policies that can impact business decisions, promoting the solution to other areas in the organization, and assisting in acquiring ongoing project funding.

The work the Agile business analyst does on behalf of the business is intended to reduce, *not eliminate*, the need for the business users to confirm whether the developed solution meets their requirements. Involving Agile business analysts in the project can substantially reduce time demands on already inundated business users, which allows them to focus what little time they have available on responding to the most important system capabilities, and on making the most crucial decisions. Not only does the involvement of Agile business analysts provide Agile developers with more timely feedback on the solution under development, it also reduces the need for business users to make a substantial upfront commitment on their availability to work on the project altogether. This can avoid having the most knowledgeable business users be hesitant to work with the Agile project team because they are concerned it will require too much of their already limited time.

The involvement of the Agile business analyst is not only a time saver for the business users; Agile business analysts can undertake several activities to assist the Agile developers in their ongoing analysis, design, and delivery work, which can provide them with more time to focus on their development work. This includes identifying data mapping, conversion, and migration requirements; analyzing interface requirements for external systems; investigating legacy systems; identifying permissions and security requirements; advising on capacity planning; and assisting in asset and infrastructure acquisition.

These are some of the 30 core activities an Agile business analyst can do to provide immediate and ongoing value to the Agile development team, as detailed in the following chapter.

CHAPTER 5: 30 WAYS FOR THE AGILE BUSINESS ANALYST TO ADD VALUE TO YOUR PROJECT

The previous chapters identified some of the critical (and often hidden) exposures in Agile approaches, both in the limited ongoing availability of the business users, and in the potential for the delivered solution to be skewed to meet the needs of only a subset of the intended user base. In particular, these chapters emphasized the need for the Agile world to strongly consider the *pairing* of business users to be as important in ensuring the *business integrity* of the solution as it is in ensuring the *technical integrity*.

Although the value the Agile business analyst can bring to solution delivery begins with their ability to work directly with the business users to confirm their requirements, there is significantly more value the Agile business analyst can bring to all aspects of project work. The following section details 30 activities an Agile business analyst can undertake throughout the project to assist the team, and to substantially increase the relevance, usability, and quality of the delivered solution.

1. Identifying and confirming user stories

User stories are part of an Agile approach that helps shift the focus from writing about requirements to talking about them. – Mike Cohn[1]

If the Agile project has not yet begun, the ideal role for the Agile business analyst is to work with the business users on

---

1 Source: *www.mountaingoatsoftware.com/topics/user-stories.*

identifying and documenting the user stories that represent their desired system behavior, as input to the initial discussions with the development team. This not only provides the Agile business analyst with hands-on awareness of the objectives of the solution from the users' perspectives, it allows the business users and the Agile business analyst to work together on:

- assigning business values to requested capabilities
- assessing the impact of requested capabilities on business processes, procedures, and policies (e.g. security restrictions)
- identifying any documentation, training, or ongoing support requirements for requested capabilities.

It also forms the basis for the ongoing relationship between the business users and the Agile business analyst that will be critical throughout the project, particularly if the Agile business analyst is needed to serve as a proxy for the business users because they are unavailable (see *Providing business continuity for the Agile developers* for further detail). Having firsthand knowledge of the business drivers for each requested capability also enables the Agile business analyst to better assist the Agile team in making decisions about the user interfaces and system behavior in the development work.

If the team is at a midway point in the Agile project, the Agile business analyst can use the existing user stories (completed and pending) as a basis for the initial discussions with the business users, both to confirm intended system behavior and to retrospectively consider the business value, impacts, and supporting needs for each requested capability.

As part of these discussions, the Agile business analyst can also begin initial investigations into areas that may be impacted by the requested capabilities, including:

- data required from legacy or third-party systems
- detailed validation and business rules
- network and infrastructure requirements
- costs and lead time for purchasing equipment
- security and permissions requirements
- systems integration requirements
- impacts on organizational KPIs and management reporting.

This information can provide greater input into the assignment of business values for each requested feature (e.g. in order to be able to use this feature, we would need $12,000 to upgrade the barcode scanners in the warehouse); as well as the estimation and planning work done by the Agile development team (e.g. the interchange feature cannot be delivered without changes to web services in the current payroll system that would require at least four months of development work).

2. Assessing the business value and priority of each capability

In the previous section, it was identified that it can be difficult for business users, even the most well-intentioned ones, to be sufficiently objective to:

- see beyond their current business practices
- equally weight the needs of *their* business area against the needs identified by other stakeholders
- forego (or scale back) a requested feature that can provide a significant benefit to their own work.

Inevitably, this limited ability for business users to completely separate themselves from the requested capabilities creates a risk that the delivered solution will be skewed to meet the needs of only a *subset* of the intended user base. It also creates the potential for the business user to escalate the priority of those features that would most greatly benefit *their* work against those that would provide more benefit to the organization overall.

It is important to emphasize that the skewing of priorities in a feature list is rarely a *conscious* decision on the part of the business users. It is simply human nature for people to be drawn to – and to place a greater value on – the things with which they are most familiar. The challenge is in getting business users to see beyond their personal knowledge and preferences, in order to *objectively* assess the relative business value of requested features. An Agile business analyst is in a position to bring a level of objectivity in the assessment and valuation of requested features that the people who have a direct stake in the outcomes often cannot.

One of the primary goals of Agile approaches is to provide the organization with the *most valuable solution* achievable in the allocated time and budget. In order to achieve this goal, the capabilities selected for development in each iteration of Agile development need to be the ones that will genuinely deliver the greatest *business-value return*[2] to the users, the business areas, and the organization.

2 Business value return is the value generated by the capability minus the overhead costs of delivering that capability. This can be measured as quantitative value (e.g. revenue generation, reduced staff time) or qualitative value (e.g. employee satisfaction).

This business-value return can take on several forms, including:

- increased revenue
- increased profit margins
- reduced overheads
- increased service delivery
- more effective service delivery
- better customer service
- increased employee satisfaction
- higher-quality outputs
- reduced risk
- greater market awareness
- a more positive image of your organization in the marketplace.

It is reasonable to assume that every requested feature in a solution is able to deliver one or more of the business-value returns in the previous list to some degree. However, when your project has limited time, budget, or resources to deliver everything on the list (as most projects do), it is important to make the distinction between those features that can provide *a moderate degree of business-value return* to the organization, and those features that can deliver *the most significant business-value return.*

The prioritization of items on the feature list should be based on what capabilities will deliver the greatest business-value returns on the project, not on personal preferences, on appeasing the most vocal stakeholders, or on other *subjective* drivers that can deliberately – or unintentionally – influence the priority order assigned by the business users.

The Agile business analyst is able to work with the business users to ensure that:

- every requested item on the feature list is assigned an *expected business value*[3] based on both the quantitative and qualitative returns it can deliver
- the assigned expected business value for each item on the feature list is used as the *primary basis* for creating the initial priority order of requested capabilities that is brought to the iteration planning session
- once the Agile development team has reviewed the business users' highest-priority requested capabilities, and provided estimates for the amount of work required to deliver these items, the business users then *reassess* their original business-value calculations to factor in the *overhead cost* of delivering the requested capability.

The activity described in the last preceding bullet point may be a new approach for some Agile practitioners. For many Agile project teams, the original priority list provided by the business users is gospel. The question is not *whether* these features will deliver the greatest business-value return to the organization, but *how many* of these high-priority features can be reasonably delivered within the iteration timeframe.

There is, however, a strong argument to say the *amount of effort* required to deliver a requested capability is an equally important factor in assessing the true business-value return of that capability. For example, the business users may

---

3 See *Everything you want to know about Agile* for detailed instructions on how to assign expected business values to individual features in a solution.

provide the Agile development team with a feature list that has the following top-down priorities:

- Provide banking customers with summary statements of their total credits, debits, and pending transactions for a specified date range.
- Allow banking customers to view scanned images of checks that have been posted against their accounts.
- Display new notifications from the bank in bold text at the top of the screen.
- Display time stamps with each transaction.
- ...

In assessing this work, the Agile developers estimate that:

- the first item on the feature list (summary statements) will take 26 *units of work*[4] to complete
- the second item on the feature list (scanned images of checks) will take 48 *units of work* to complete
- the third item on the feature list (new bank notifications display) will take 12 *units of work* to complete
- the fourth item on the feature list (time stamp display) will take 10 *units of work* to complete.

The velocity[5] of the Agile development team on previous iterations indicates they can commit to a maximum of *50 units of work per iteration.* From a scheduling standpoint,

---

4 Units of work represent the relative expected effort needed for the team to deliver a feature (e.g. One for simple features, five for complex features). It is primarily used for estimation purposes.

5 Velocity is a measurement of historical productivity levels that allows Agile project teams to confidently make estimations of the effort required for future work.

this would mean the business users have the option of either:

- getting the first item on the feature list, and then breaking down the second item on the feature list (where possible) to a subset of the capability that can be delivered in the remaining 24 units of work (e.g. show each posted check as a 'virtual' check image)
- getting the first item on the feature list, and then postponing the development of the second item on the feature list in favor of getting both the third and fourth items in the next iteration.

There is, however, more for the business users to consider than the scheduling.

The estimates provided by the Agile developers not only provide the business users with input on *how many items* can be delivered for each iteration but also provide input into *how much effort (overhead)* is required to deliver each capability. With this information in hand, the business users are in a position to *reassess* their original expected business-value calculations for each item, and confirm the extent to which the delivery costs may diminish the business-value return for each requested item.

In this example, the business users had assessed 'scanned images of checks' to be the second item on the initial feature list based on the originally calculated expected business value for that capability. Now that the Agile team has estimated it would take 48 units of work for this capability to be developed, the business users know it would take an *entire iteration worth of effort* to deliver this one capability. With this knowledge, they are in a position to reconsider whether the business-value return of this capability justifies its development cost.

The Agile business analyst can assist the business users, both in the original calculation of the expected business value of each item on the feature list and in the re-calculation – and reprioritization – of the business-value returns for these items once the Agile development team has provided its estimates.

Where an originally requested feature is determined to have a business-value return that *does not* justify its development, the Agile business analyst and the Agile developers can assist the business users in identifying *viable alternative options* to support the intended business objective of that capability. This can include both alternative functionality within the software, as well as business process changes and other workarounds that do not require the same degree of development work.

It should be noted that the final decision on what capabilities should – and should not – be included in each iteration is not as simple as drawing a line and only focusing on the items above that line. In some cases, it makes sense for the Agile development team to 'cherry-pick' capabilities from lower down in the feature list where they are directly related to the higher-priority capabilities being delivered, particularly where the added overhead of delivering these additional features is minimal. For example, a high-priority item at the top of an online ordering system list may be to make the 'shopping cart' feature automatically recalculate total amounts when a product quantity is changed. A corresponding item lower on that list may be to default the quantity to '1' whenever a new product is added to the shopping cart. In undertaking this work, the development team may determine that changing the default quantity to '1' is a simple fix to a code value in the shopping cart module that can be updated at the same time the higher-priority change is being made.

It should also be noted that items deferred earlier on in the project because the delivery costs were too high can be *revisited* by the business users and the Agile development team at a future point to see if more recent updates to the system (e.g. the incorporation of a third-party reporting tool or searching utility) can reduce the amount of work required to deliver this capability.

3. *Finding viable alternatives to satisfy business requirements*

The previous section identified *business-value returns* as the primary driver to use in the determination of what capabilities the solution will deliver, and in what priority order. In the example given, one of the originally requested capabilities (scanned images of checks) was determined to be too costly to deliver in the current system. The decision to remove this capability from the features list (or to move it farther down on the list) addressed the need to focus Agile development work on the highest business-value return capabilities, but it *did not* address the originally identified business requirement to provide banking customers with an easy way of viewing and reconciling the checks posted against their accounts.

As described in *Chapter 4: What are the Risks of Not Having an Agile Business Analyst*, one of the primary values an Agile business analyst can bring to the project is helping business users determine the best way to satisfy each business requirement, whether it is resolved as: a system feature; a change to the business processes, procedures, and policies outside of the system; or a combination of these.

For the example provided in the previous section, it was determined that 'scanned images of checks' in its originally described form cannot be delivered cost-effectively in the current system. With this information in hand, the Agile business analyst is able to work with the business users to determine if there are changes that can be delivered *outside of the system* – or if there are more cost-effective variations on this capability that can be delivered *within the system* – which will sufficiently address the originally identified business requirement.

The Agile business analyst would generally start this analysis by confirming with the business users exactly what is driving the overall requirement for providing banking customers with images of their checks. For example, this requirement could have been driven by:

- a regulatory mandate for all financial institutions to provide customers with the details for any check debited against their funds
- a corporate 'transparency' policy, which states all customers must be able to clearly and easily see the details for all of the credit and debit transactions applied to their accounts
- a response to feedback received from the customer-service department that customers are unhappy with how difficult it is to identify what checks have – and have not – been cleared against their accounts
- a management directive based on operational reports that identified it takes 320 staff hours per year to

address customer questions about which specific checks have cleared against their accounts.

Any one of these four drivers (or a combination of them) could have originally resulted in the business users presenting the Agile development team with the following user story:

As a banking customer, I want an easy way of viewing the checks posted against my account, so I can confirm whether the checks are valid and keep track of available funds.

Further discussion between the business users and the Agile development team in the iteration planning session indicated the best way to address this requirement would be to add scanned images of checks to the account details screens. As the development cost for this approach was seen to be too high, however, it was determined an alternative approach may need to be considered. The decision on what alternative approach would sufficiently address the requirement – and whether the requirement *must* be addressed altogether – really depends on which of the previous bullet point(s) is driving it.

Where the driver of the requirement is a regulatory mandate, the organization has no choice but to find a resolution that *reasonably adheres to* that mandate. The following section (*Ensuring compliance with regulations and mandates*) addresses how the Agile business analyst can help the business users to work within these mandates.

Similarly, when the driver of the requirement is a corporate policy, the business users may have limited (or no) discretion on whether the project team can omit this requirement from the solution. See *Adhering to corporate policies* for guidelines on how to address these constraints.

If the requirement is being driven by the business areas or internal management, the business users are likely to have greater flexibility to use alternative approaches to address it (or to put forward a reasonable business case to management) than they would have in the previous two circumstances. More detail on this is provided in *Reviewing and refining existing business processes*.

Note that the activities described in this section do not need to wait for a requested capability to be taken off of (or to be moved down) the feature list. The Agile business analyst can equally assist the business users in proactively assessing alternative options for each capability as part of the initial gathering of requirements for the feature list, and in the consideration of the highest-priority capabilities in each subsequent iteration. In some cases, this assessment can provide the business users with a viable, more cost-effective alternative for a capability everyone had previously assumed would be addressed in the software. In other cases, this assessment can result in *a range of approaches* for addressing the requirement in the solution, which can then be discussed with the Agile development team to determine the most technically achievable approach with the most manageable overheads.

4. Ensuring compliance with regulations and mandates

If a requested capability *must* be delivered by the project team due to external mandates (e.g. government regulations), then the question for the business users to address is not *whether* the capability will be included, but *how* it will be. Where many business users may see a mandate as a black-and-white directive, the Agile business analyst has the objectivity to step away from the literal interpretation of the mandate to identify potential alternatives and workarounds that would still provide compliance, but would not require significant enhancements to the solution in development.

In the example provided, the following was identified as the mandate that prompted the requested 'scanned images of checks' capability:

All financial institutions must provide customers with the details for any check debited against their funds.

Upon closer inspection of the wording of the mandate, the Agile business analyst advises the business users that there is no specific requirement to provide check details *online*, only that the details must be available to them, which could be via other channels (e.g. phone support, photocopies sent via standard mail). Equally, there is no mandate that this information must be provided *proactively*. All the banking institution needs in order to be compliant with the mandate is to be able to provide check details in response to a customer request.

The end result of this investigation is that compliance with the regulation need not be addressed in the software. Although providing the 'scanned images of checks' capability in the solution is likely to deliver operational efficiencies and customer-service advantages for the organization, it is left to the discretion of the business users to assess whether there are other capabilities that can be delivered in the software which would deliver an even greater business-value return for the organization.

Where mandates are imposing unreasonable or unachievable demands on the solution, the Agile business analyst is also able to assist the project team by one or both of the following:

- Reviewing the complete mandate to determine if there are any acceptable alternative approaches stated.
- Researching how similar organizations in the industry have addressed this requirement.

Investigating these mandates is work that could reasonably be done by other members of the Agile team, if they had the time and the background knowledge, but the developers generally rely upon the business users to undertake these activities. Similarly, the business users could do this research on their own, but many will not have the time to undertake a thorough investigation; without being prompted by the Agile business analyst, they may not even be aware there is flexibility in the application of these regulations.

The following sections identify how the Agile business analyst can further assist the project team when the resolution requires changes to policies or to business processes in the organization.

5. Adhering to corporate policies

Another potential driver identified for including the 'scanned images of checks' capability in the solution was adherence with the following corporate policy:

The "transparency" policy, which states that all customers must be able to clearly and easily see the details for all of the credit and debit transactions applied to their accounts.

Unlike the regulatory mandate described in the previous section, this corporate policy is much more specific about the minimum customer-service requirements the organization must adhere to. In particular, the term 'clearly and easily see the details' has two implications: the channel for accessing these details must be visual (i.e. not verbally advised to the customer via phone support), and the presentation must be 'clear and easy' for the customer to understand.

As with the regulatory mandate, the assessment undertaken by the Agile business analyst identifies that there is nothing in the preceding corporate policy that requires the resolution to be addressed in the software. There are, however, fewer alternative options that provide this information in a visual format that is easy for customers to access. Both of the previously identified business workarounds (phone support and/or photocopies sent via standard mail) may not be sufficient for the resolution to be considered compliant with the policy.

In this situation, the Agile business analyst can suggest a few alternatives to the business users:

- Brainstorm with the Agile developers on whether there is a more cost-effective way to make check details available within the software. One example may be changing the capability to an 'on demand' feature that sends a request notification to a staff member, who then manually scans the requested checks and posts them on the banking customer's account details screen.
- Approach the staff in the organization who are responsible for developing and enforcing corporate policies to identify how much room for interpretation there is in the policy. (i.e. would sending photocopies of checks via standard mail be considered an 'easy' way for customers to get these details?)
- Recommend an update to the corporate policy wording that allows for other delivery channels (e.g. phone

support) to be considered compliant (noting that changes to corporate policies can often take months to be approved and issued).

- Ask management (or the project executive) to permit an exception to the corporate policy, based on the estimated delivery cost of this feature.

Depending on the nature of the organization, it may be possible for the Agile team to recommend an approach that adheres to the *spirit* of the corporate policy (i.e. its intent), even if it does not adhere to the *letter* of the policy (i.e. the exact wording). The Agile business analyst can work with the business users on positioning an appropriate argument to the decision makers to get approval for alternative approaches that achieve the organization's customer-service objectives without handcuffing the capabilities in the solution.

6. Reviewing and refining existing business processes

The two previous sections identified situations where a requested capability was being driven by corporate policy or by regulatory compliance – and where there appeared to be limited opportunity for the Agile team members to use their discretion in excluding this capability, even if delivering it would use an inordinate percentage of the available project resources.

This section deals with a somewhat different challenge: a capability requested to address an *internal business driver* in the organization. The two drivers identified in the previous example are based on the following:

- Feedback received from the customer-service department that customers are unhappy with how difficult it is to identify what checks have – and have not – been cleared against their accounts.

- A management directive based on operational reports that identified it takes 320 staff hours per year to address customer questions about which specific checks have cleared against their accounts.

The Agile business analyst can help the business users get to the heart of the business drivers, and separate the originally requested capability from other available options that may be able to equally (or possibly better) address this business requirement. For example, it may be possible to provide customers with scanned images of their checks *without* needing to display these images as part of the online banking screens. Two alternative ways to achieve this could be by:

- Providing a report that the customer can link to which summarizes all of their processed checks for the stated period.
- Proactively including scanned check images in printed statements, which can minimize the need for customers to get this information from the online system.

The organization may also be able to reduce the overheads associated with processing checks by making their internal workflows more efficient, for example:

- Changing the incoming mail procedures to make it easier for checks to be scanned, and for the scanned check images to be automatically uploaded to the server that hosts the online banking application.

Although this business process change would not fulfill the requirement for providing customers with the ability to see their posted checks, it could reduce backend operational costs. Having the scanned images directly on the server can also make it easier for the Agile development team to build capabilities to access these images without needing to build (and test) separate interfaces, which can reduce the amount of effort required for the team to deliver this capability.

The involvement of the Agile business analyst in addressing these business drivers may also result in proposed business changes that have little to do with building capabilities in the software solution or with changing the internal business processes, for example:

- Recommending that the organization encourages more customers to use electronic funds transfers for bill payments, etc. to reduce the volume of paper checks processed overall.

All of the preceding options can allow the organization to achieve its customer service and operational cost management objectives without depending upon the software solution as the only mechanism for delivering these outcomes.

Skilled Agile business analysts can use a number of techniques to identify where existing business processes can be made more efficient, including:

- *Business process modeling and business process optimization*, which involves documenting the current business processes an organization uses and assessing them to determine where inefficiencies exist. One of the most effective ways of modeling business processes is by using business process modeling notation

(BPMN)[6], which is an industry standard for documenting business processes in visual diagrams with supporting textual information.

- *Applying Lean techniques* that focus on *waste management* in order to address the most common inefficiencies in business processes, such as over-handling, decentralized information, serial tasks, over-management, and overuse of decision points (see the *Lean* section of *Chapter 8: More Information on Agile* for resources that detail these inefficiencies).
- *Baselining and measuring* that involves assessing and recording the business value of work activities *prior to* the introduction of proposed improvements in order to measure comparative quantitative and qualitative gains.
- *Using predictive analysis techniques* to model proposed future changes before they are implemented. This involves a combination of baselining current work activities, and then documenting alternative business process models with metrics to demonstrate where time and resource efficiencies would occur.

These techniques allow the Agile business analyst to objectively review existing business processes, to identify potential areas of improvement, and to recommend adjustments, where needed, with supporting documentation. Not only can this work assist the business users (and the Agile team) in seeing alternative options to delivering efficiencies exclusively in the software; these techniques can be applied to model the business processes that will be used when the system is implemented, allowing the

---

6 For more details on Business Process Modeling, go to the Object Management Group's Business Process Model and Notation website (*www.bpmn.org/*).

organization to best leverage the capabilities of the delivered solution in ongoing operations.

7. Getting input from all relevant stakeholders

It would be a logistical nightmare (if not an impossibility) for the Agile team to work directly with *every stakeholder* who may be impacted by the developed solution. Unless the Agile team is building a niche solution that is targeted for only a small number of users, it is inevitable there will be a broad range of people who have a vested interest in the delivered solution. The business users who have the primary responsibility for identifying and prioritizing the solution requirements generally only represent *a portion* of these stakeholders. If time allows, these business users may be in a position to consult with broader audiences and incorporate their feedback in the prioritized features list. More often than not, however, the business users are only able to speak with a subset of these additional stakeholders. This is another area where the Agile business analyst is able to assist the business users, particularly those who want to ensure the delivered solution will be well-received across the organization, but who are not in a position to gather information from the relevant stakeholders themselves.

Involving the additional stakeholders can occur at several points in the project timeline:

- In the requirements-gathering activities that occur prior to the initial discussions with the Agile development team, to ensure the scope of the solution and the priorities in the features list reflect their interests, as well as those of the primary business users.
- At each iteration, where the stakeholders may not be able to attend the walkthrough of the developed

software, the Agile business analyst can take them through the system separately, and gather their feedback for consideration by the primary business users in their ongoing requirements identification and prioritization.

- Prior to the live release of the solution, to make them more comfortable with the capabilities being delivered, which can assist in encouraging the use of the system and gaining their support.
- After the live release of the solution to determine if they are satisfied with the solution, and to identify potential areas for improvement.

Assigning an Agile business analyst to undertake these activities not only frees the business users to focus on their other responsibilities, it may provide a forum where other stakeholders are able to speak more freely about their concerns. This is a situation where the work the Agile business analyst undertakes has both operational benefits for the organization and political benefits for the Agile team. The more involvement these stakeholders have throughout the project timeline, the more amenable they will be to using – and to supporting – the system when it is released. Conversely, when stakeholders feel as though they have been *neglected* in the process, they are likely to be much more resistant to using – and critical of – the delivered solution. Getting widespread and vocal support for the solution is not only important for the Agile team, it may also be a crucial step in getting ongoing funding for future work on the solution, as well as support for the continued use of Agile approaches in the organization overall.

8. Managing feature lists and priorities

For most Agile methods, business users are not only responsible for identifying and documenting their requested system features, they are responsible for *prioritizing* – and for *re-prioritizing* – these capabilities throughout the project, in order to provide the Agile development team with a clear understanding of the highest-priority features the solution needs to deliver at each stage.

Generally, the responsibility for prioritizing system features is left exclusively for the business users to undertake on their own *prior to* meeting with the Agile development team. These features are then presented to the developers as a top-down prioritized list (e.g. a product backlog[7]) for discussion, estimation, and planning. Agile methods tend to work from the assumption that business users understand the value of each requested capability far better than the development team does and are, therefore, in the best position to identify the most critical features. There are, however, some key flaws in this logic:

- Business users, even the most well-intentioned ones, tend to favor those features that benefit their position and their work area the most. This can make prioritization a somewhat biased activity with few counter-balances to confirm whether the assigned priorities accurately reflect the best interests of the other user groups, or the organization overall.

---

7 The term 'product backlog' is most closely associated with the Scrum method, but could be equally applied to any prioritized list of system features presented to the Agile development team for estimation.

- When there is one individual (e.g. a product owner) who is responsible for representing the interests of all business users, this bias becomes even more evident. It is inevitable that this one representative will have greater knowledge, awareness, and empathy for the requirements of some user groups and business areas than others.
- The assessment and assignment of 'priority work' can be subjective, primarily based on the business users' perspectives of what constitutes a *high-priority feature*. For some business users, a high-priority feature is one that will most substantially reduce operational overheads for the organization; for others, a high-priority feature is the one they receive the most complaints about; and, for others still, a high-priority feature is the one that has the greatest appeal to senior management.
- In assessing priorities, business users may not factor in other considerations that could impact the relative value of requested features, such as:
    - potential business process changes and other workarounds that could have minimized or negated the need for the requested feature altogether
    - Any materials (e.g. training, documentation) or additional resources that may be needed to support the new feature in day-to-day operations
    - The ongoing cost of maintaining the requested feature when the system is in the live environment.

As Agile methods are specifically designed to deliver the *highest business-value solution* to the organization, it is important to consider the potential impact of all of these variables in the prioritization and management of requested features. Accurately assigning priorities to requested system features can, however, be a difficult thing for any business user (even the most experienced ones) to do without assistance from an objective 'third party' who can review, question, and, where needed, challenge these priorities. This is where Agile business analysts are particularly valuable resources, as they have reasonable levels of business knowledge, technical knowledge, and, most importantly, the *objectivity* to work with the business users to ensure that assigned priorities reflect – and continue to reflect – the full range of variables previously identified.

The Agile business analyst is able to provide support to the business users as part of the initial identification, valuation, and prioritization of items on the feature list, and throughout the project timeline, particularly in preparation for each subsequent iteration planning session with the Agile development team.

9. Providing input to Agile team estimation and planning

Once the prioritized list of requested features has been discussed with the Agile development team, the team then uses this information as input into their estimation and planning for the next iteration of project work. The Agile business analyst can assist in these activities in two ways:

- Like every Agile team member, the Agile business analyst can provide their estimations of the work required, factoring in the knowledge gained from their hands-on work with the business users.
- Any initial investigation work done by the Agile business analyst on data migration, systems integration, security, infrastructure, and other dependencies is information the Agile development team can use to make their estimates more accurate.

For example, the Agile development team needs to estimate the amount of work required to deliver the following feature:

As a manager, I want to be able to see how much annual vacation time each employee in my department has so I can more accurately plan for staff shortages.

With only this information in hand, the team is likely to base their estimates on the amount of work required to:

- use the manager's user profile to determine which employees work in that department
- submit the employee ID numbers for that department to the human resources management system (HRMS)
- retrieve a total count of remaining vacation days from the HRMS for each employee ID
- present these details in a table view on the management reporting screens.

The Agile business analyst may, however, be able to provide the team with additional information from their initial investigation work that could make these estimates more accurate, such as:

- Due to recent cutbacks, many employees are working part-time across multiple departments, which means managers need to be able to *pro rate* the available vacation days for these employees.
- The HRMS:
  - does not currently provide a per employee summary of remaining annual vacation days through its external interfaces, or
  - is able to provide the remaining annual vacation days for each employee, but requires employee ID values to be encrypted, or

- o is scheduled to be replaced by another system in eight months.

Each of these additional pieces of information could influence the estimates provided by the team for this feature, particularly where it introduces unexpected complexities in the development or implementation work.

There is, of course, an argument to say these complexities would have eventually emerged in the development process, and would have been addressed with the business users at subsequent planning sessions. That is, in fact, exactly why Agile methods focus on making solutions adaptable to unexpected constraints and hurdles that arise in the development process. While this is true, there is an equally compelling argument to say it is in the best interest of the project team – and the organization – for *known risks* to be identified as early as possible in the process to avoid having the team make decisions (even estimates) based on incomplete or inaccurate information.

In many respects, the role of the Agile business analyst is to assist the Agile team by identifying potential business and system risk factors *as early as possible*. This empowers the team to make more accurate estimates, provides more lead time to address identified hurdles, and provides business users with a better understanding of why a feature that appeared to be simple on paper is more complicated to implement than expected.

The Agile business analyst is able to investigate numerous factors that could influence the Agile development team's estimates, including:

- the quantities, locations, and permissions levels of target users

- the availability, capabilities, and constraints of legacy systems
- the volume and complexity of legacy data
- planned changes to external systems.

Once the Agile development team has provided their estimates on the top-priority items on the feature list, the Agile business analyst can further assist the business users in the *reassessment* of the originally assigned priorities for their requested capabilities, based on the *business-value return*, of each item on the list, as described in *Assessing the business value and priority of each capability*.

It should also be noted that if a feature is unrealistic or unachievable altogether, the Agile business analyst can intervene *well before* it is added to the priority list, advising business users about the constraints and working with them to identify alternative options.

10. Researching and resolving outstanding issues

As described in the previous section, the Agile business analyst is able to assist the Agile team from the very start of the project, by owning and investigating issues identified in the initial requirements-gathering activities – as well as issues that arise in the subsequent planning and estimation discussions with the Agile development team. There are, however, several other points throughout the project where the Agile business analyst can provide invaluable assistance to address issues in order to free up the development team and progress project work. This includes:

- Clarification of detailed requirements during the development process, from confirmation of screen layouts, flows, and field names, to validation rules, to desired system behavior. In some cases, the Agile business analyst will have this information available, based on their collaborative work with the business users. In other cases, the Agile business analyst can take ownership of discussing the developers' questions with the relevant business users, or arrange to have the business users view the 'in progress' system firsthand to provide their feedback. Either way, the Agile business analyst can expedite the process and allow the team to make development decisions more quickly.

- Investigation of constraints before and during the development process, such as third party and legacy system capabilities, legacy data structures, key resource availability, network limitations, hardware and equipment availability, etc., as well as organizational policy and procedural limitations.
- Follow up on issues from iterative review sessions where further information (or confirmation) is needed for selected features to be progressed in the next iteration. This includes background investigation to confirm the business value of proposed new features, or to consider alternative approaches (e.g. business process changes, staff training) that may negate the need for the new feature altogether.

In many cases, these issues could be addressed by the developers themselves, but that would take precious time away from their development work. Alternatively, a team facilitator (e.g. a ScrumMaster) could take ownership of these issues, but may not be as well positioned as the Agile business analyst to address issues related to business requirements, constraints, or valuation of features.

Where issues are particularly time-consuming to address because they require further research (e.g. gathering metrics) or because they require consensus from a range of stakeholders, it is extremely valuable to have an Agile business analyst take ownership of the issue and minimize distractions to other Agile team members, including the team facilitator.

11. Assisting Agile team members in designing user interfaces

All of the activities covered in this section until now have focused on what the Agile business analyst is able to do to assist the business users in the identification, confirmation, and valuation of the *business requirements* for the solution. There is, however, an equally important role the Agile business analyst is able to play to assist the Agile team in their *software development* and *implementation* work. The following describes these development-related activities, including how they are able to provide the Agile developers with more time to focus on building and delivering the solution.

The value of the Agile business analyst is not only in responding to questions that arise while the Agile developers are building the system; the Agile business analyst is also able to work hands-on with the developers in the initial and ongoing *solution design*, particularly in the design of screen layouts and screen flows.

Agile business analysts do not only bring objectivity and firsthand knowledge of business requirements to the design discussion, based on their hands-on work with the business users. Many of them are formally trained in software usability and accessibility guidelines, which can create a valuable pairing opportunity with the developers.

This means the Agile developers get the benefit of an 'on-call' business representative to work with them throughout the design process, and the Agile business analyst is better positioned to address business user perceived usability issues in acceptance testing and training because of their direct involvement in the design decisions.

This approach is also beneficial for those Agile developers who are more comfortable adapting a proposed screen layout than starting with a blank screen. The Agile business analyst can provide an overall framework for the interface as a starting point for the Agile developer to work from, and then assist them in the ongoing extension and refinement of the initially designed screens.

12. Analyzing data mapping, conversion, and migration requirements

Assisting in the interface design is not the only way the Agile business analyst is able to support the Agile team during the development process. When the system being developed requires data from other systems (e.g. legacy systems, third-party solutions) the business analyst is able to undertake data analysis and preliminary work for the data migration and/or ongoing data interchange.

This work can include:

- field mappings
- value list mappings
- data sampling
- data validation
- data cleansing

- identifying and resolving orphan records
- test migrations
- metrics for source and target systems.

Not only does this reduce the amount of work the developers need to focus on, it can also provide the team with initial testing of the proposed data structures in the developed system, as well as an opportunity to confirm whether system functions and screen designs work as expected with populated data.

If there are issues or complexities with the data in the source system, the Agile business analyst can initiate discussions with the relevant areas as early as possible to minimize their impact on ongoing development work.

In most cases, Agile business analysts will not be in a position to build the data migration applications, but the analysis work they do can assist the Agile development team in testing, refining, and fixing these applications before they are released.

13. Analyzing interface requirements for external systems

Similar to providing assistance on data migration activities, the Agile business analyst can also assist the Agile development team in investigating the requirements for interfacing with external systems, including legacy systems and third-party solutions. This can include identifying available fields and formats for interchange, validation rules, communication protocols, encryption algorithms, and scheduling parameters.

This is another area where preliminary work done by the Agile business analyst can help to identify and address risks to the project before they become substantial issues. It is also an area where the Agile business analyst can undertake preliminary testing (and setting up of test data) to confirm interface capabilities and constraints.

As with data migration, it is unlikely Agile business analysts will be able to build the interchange functions for the solution, but their analysis work can provide the development team with *achievable* specifications.

Where external systems are managed by other areas of the organization, or by service providers, there is likely to be a need to coordinate activities between the teams to establish agreed specifications, progress any required development work, undertake unit testing of individual interfaces, and conduct full integration testing. The Agile business analyst is able to work with these external groups to coordinate these activities and to follow up on any requirements-related and technical questions raised as work progresses.

14. Investigating legacy systems

Where the solution being developed by the Agile team is *replacing* one or more existing systems, the Agile business analyst can assist both the business users and the Agile developers by undertaking a thorough review of the current systems in order to:

- Determine the scope of existing functionality as input into requirements discussions with the business users. Note that this is as much an exercise in ensuring the newly developed solution includes all necessary capabilities, as it is in confirming with the business areas why previous capabilities *are not* being included in the new solution – and whether corresponding operational changes may be needed to compensate for these omitted capabilities.

- Identify the legacy systems' existing integration points with external systems, as input into the activities described in *Analyzing interface requirements for external systems*. This presents the Agile developers with an opportunity for 'piggybacking' on integration interfaces that may already exist. It also provides another confirmation of whether the business users have factored in all of the relevant capabilities from the legacy systems in the scope of the new solution.
- Analyze legacy data structures and record values. As described in *Analyzing data mapping, conversion, and migration requirements*, any newly developed system is likely to require some degree of pre-population with legacy system data. The Agile business analyst's review of legacy system behavior, storage structures, and data utilization can provide the Agile development team with a better understanding of what functions the data supports in the legacy system (e.g. reporting), and how that data was presented to users in that system. This analysis can also help identify the purpose of encoded values and look-up lists, which can further assist in the data mapping and migration work.
- Assess when the legacy systems can be safely *decommissioned*, including whether the systems (or select capabilities within the systems) need to remain available in a restricted mode (e.g. read-only) for a period of time, particularly when the new system being developed by the Agile team is not replacing the full scope of existing functionality.
- Extract previous lists of user accounts and permissions as a baseline for setting up the equivalent configurations in the new solution. See *Identifying*

permissions and security requirements for further information.

- Establish comparative values for expected testing results to confirm, where appropriate, that equivalent existing functions (e.g. calculations) generate the same results in the new solution.
- Provide the Agile development team with a better understanding of the business terminology the users are familiar with, as input into their interface design.
- Position existing system behavior as a reference point for training materials, comparing the functionality users are currently familiar with against the equivalent (and updated) functionality in the new solution.

The analysis of legacy systems is also important for the Agile business analyst to confirm whether the capabilities requested by the business users are based on a well-considered approach to business operations with the new system, and not simply a redevelopment of the existing functionality because that is the approach they are used to following.

15. Identifying permissions and security requirements

One of the benefits of having the Agile business analyst review the legacy systems that the new solution is intended to replace is it provides the Agile development team with insight into the full range of existing user accounts, account settings, user roles, and user groups as the baseline for the permissions settings in the new solution. It may also be possible for the Agile business analyst to gather some of this information from other systems that the new solution is intended to integrate with, to ensure these settings are consistently applied in cross-system functionality.

The Agile business analyst's investigation of the legacy systems may also provide the team with an understanding of how granular the permission settings need to be, identifying whether they are applied to selected modules, menus, functions, records, fields, and/or field values.

Although the new solution is unlikely to have exactly the same security and permissions structures as the legacy systems, having this information in hand allows the Agile developers to assess what the equivalent levels of restrictions would be in the replacement system.

The Agile business analyst may also be able to assist in the replication of these permissions structures in the configuration of the development, test, or live environments on behalf of the team.

Similarly, there may also be a need for the Agile business analyst to investigate infrastructure security requirements for the new solution, including network restrictions, remote access limitations, encryption requirements for data storage, as well as the purchasing and installation of security certificates.

If some (or all) of the data being used by the new solution is classified, the Agile business analyst can identify where there is a requirement for the new solution to enforce permissions settings on data access requests. In highly secure environments, this investigation can also identify whether the new solution needs to support records that are only held in offline data storage.

In the investigation of integration requirements for external systems, the Agile business analyst can also advise the team on whether there are security restrictions that need to be enforced for shared functionality and data exchange with these systems.

In addition to identifying these restrictions, the Agile business analyst can investigate and summarize any relevant security policies on behalf of the team. The earlier the Agile developers are made aware of the security guidelines the solution needs to comply with, the more likely these can be built into the system architecture as an intrinsic part of the solution design.

16. Advising on capacity planning

It is important for the Agile development team to know the expected short-term and long-term projected usage of the solution as critical input in their system design, although gathering and assessing this information can be an arduous and time-consuming task. This is particularly true when the projection information available is unclear, incomplete, or contradictory, depending on which area of the organization is providing these details. (e.g. the operational users advise they have never had to process more than 20 sales orders per hour; the sales and marketing team is convinced their upcoming campaigns will increase that volume to 250 orders per hour; and the executive office has projected increases over the next five years of up to 600 orders per hour. Which of these projections should the Agile development team be designing the system to support?)

The Agile business analyst is able to investigate – and realistically assess – the current and projected future capacity requirements for the new solution, including the:

- volume of data
- volume, frequency, and timing of transactions

- quantity of both named and concurrent users
- number (and location) of installations.

In addition to speaking with relevant stakeholders, the investigation work done by the Agile business analyst can include gathering metrics from legacy system use, as well as identifying any increases in business or system activity expected to occur once the new solution is implemented in the live environment.

With all of this information in hand, the Agile business analyst can then provide the developers with realistic 'best case', 'worst case', and most likely capacity volumes for their solution design work.

This capacity planning information can assist the Agile developers in designing a system architecture and network infrastructure that can adequately support the anticipated system demand upon live release, and be extensible to support the future projected demand when needed.

These details can also assist the testers in their performance and capacity testing of the solution, including providing them with advanced notice on the data, user, workstation, or transaction volumes that need to be set up to support these activities in the test environment.

17. Assisting in asset and infrastructure acquisition

Where the solution requires the organization to acquire new equipment (e.g. servers, desktops, scanners); to purchase or upgrade software products; or to invest in updating the existing infrastructure, the purchasing process can be an extremely time-consuming activity for the team, especially in the more bureaucratic organizations.

The Agile business analyst can assist the team by:

- researching available products and costs in the marketplace
- assessing the procurement guidelines and processes for the organization, including preferred supplier lists
- getting management approval for the purchase request
- arranging for competitive bids from suppliers, where required
- organizing the purchase order and related paperwork
- tracking the orders and advising the team of expected arrival dates
- following up with the supplier if there are any issues with order fulfillment or with the products received.

Several of these activities could be handled by a project (or department) administrator, if the team has this resource available. The research of available products and follow-up on issues, however, is likely to require a member of the Agile team to assist in this work, particularly where specialist knowledge is needed to distinguish product claims from product capabilities. This is another area where any support the Agile business analyst can provide to alleviate this responsibility from the Agile developers, the better positioned they will be to focus on their development work.

Where Agile business analysts are also involved in preparing funding submissions (see *Acquiring additional and ongoing project funding*), having this product research and competitive cost information in hand – along with the capacity planning details noted earlier – can assist them in determining if there are additional costs that will need to be included in the requested budget submission to support the expected future growth in the usage of the solution. Having these funds pre-allocated (and pre-approved) can reduce a substantial amount of overhead and delays for the Agile team moving forward.

18. Developing requirements, user, and/or system documentation

Although Agile approaches favor face-to-face communication over piles of documentation, there is rarely a software development project that can be delivered without any documentation whatsoever, particularly where there is an ongoing need to support users and systems administrators, as well as organizational compliance and management requirements. Creating documentation is rarely the preferred activity for most Agile developers, but, if it is a requirement of the project team, it has to be done. This is another area where the Agile business analyst can assist the Agile team, which is a responsibility most developers will happily hand over!

Where documentation (such as external system interface specifications) is required for the project, particularly where the team does not have access to a technical writer, this task can – and should – be given to the Agile business analyst. Agile business analysts are able to combine their knowledge about the system in development with their hands-on awareness of the needs of the audience for each document. In many cases, the Agile business analyst will have prior experience in writing solution documentation, including user guides, training materials, detailed validation rules, and technical support manuals, which makes them ideally suited for this work.

Depending on what other activities the Agile business analyst undertakes for the team, there may also be an opportunity for *consolidation of effort* across their tasks.

For example, an Agile business analyst who is involved in preliminary acceptance testing may be able to take screen captures of the system during the testing process, which can then be used within the user documentation. Similarly, any initial work the Agile business analyst does to provide detailed specifications and supporting materials to the Agile development team (e.g. report templates, validation rules) can be deliberately structured to fit into a post-implementation user manual or systems administration guide. If the Agile business analyst is also undertaking user and system administration training activities, this is another opportunity to build documentation, including online documentation, which is designed to serve both purposes.

The involvement of the Agile business analyst across multiple activities on the Agile team, including documentation, also provides them with the opportunity to continually view – and review – the solution from the end-user's perspective. This can reinforce their ability to objectively review the software in development, to continually advise the business users on the highest business-value capabilities, to assist the testers in focusing their work on the most critical functionality in the system, and to help structure training materials around those capabilities the users really need in the solution in order to be able to most effectively do their day-to-day work. Where Agile business analysts are involved in putting together multiple documents for the Agile team, they are also better positioned to recognize opportunities for reuse of materials across these documents, which can save the overhead costs of producing and maintaining these documents.

19. Assisting in project management reporting

In the same way Agile projects are generally required to produce some level of documentation to meet organizational compliance and post-implementation requirements, the Agile project team is often required to product project documentation that complies with the project management frameworks supported by the organization (e.g. PRINCE2®, PMBOK). This can include highlight reports, executive summaries, budget reports, contract amendments, issue logs, staff reports (e.g. leave logs, performance management), and other artifacts specific to each framework. Where the Agile team has a dedicated project manager, the Agile business analyst can assist the project manager in gathering the information required for these reports and, where required, in preparing the reports for submission. Where the Agile team does not have a dedicated project manager, and these tasks are divided among the Agile team members, the Agile business analyst can take responsibility for the majority of this work. It is expected that Agile team members will continue to provide updates on their day-to-day work through backlogs (or equivalent), but the involvement of the Agile business analyst means they do not need to worry about the overall tracking of resources, budget utilization, or other project management metrics.

The production of project management deliverables is another area where a team facilitator (e.g. a ScrumMaster) could act as the project manager on behalf of the team, creating and maintaining these documents to free up the Agile team members to focus on their primary work. As this can be a rather time-consuming activity, particularly at the end of the month, the quarter, and the financial year, any assistance the Agile business analyst can provide would relieve the team facilitator of having this work be a full-time role for them during these intense reporting periods.

20. Ensuring compliance with quality management systems

Where an organization requires projects to be compliant with their quality management system (QMS), the Agile business analyst is able to assist the team in fulfilling these requirements, including producing the following audit information:

- Comparison of the team's day-to-day work against the documented Agile practices of the organization.
- Compilation of the measurements from Agile tools, such as backlogs, burndown charts, and executive dashboards (see *Chapter 8: More Information on Agile* for resources that describe the purpose and use of specific Agile tools).
- Reporting on defects and resolutions through the artifacts the Agile teams already produce (e.g. automated testing logs and issues lists).
- Compilation of the documented outcomes from iterative review sessions with the business users.

Where needed, the Agile business analyst is able to organize interviews with system users, external business users, and management as confirmation of the effectiveness of Agile approaches.

The Agile business analyst can also assist in QMS compliance by producing documentation that describes the Agile team's current practices to establish a more consistent, clearly described, and replicable model that can be used by the organization for other project teams, for training new hires, and for educating partner organizations.

21. Documenting test plans and test cases

Most Agile teams will have professional software testers available to them, either as dedicated Agile team members, or as allocated resources in another area of the organization they can call upon as needed.

Where the Agile team is fortunate enough to have dedicated testers, the role of the Agile business analyst in developing test cases and test plans is likely to be a supporting one, assisting the dedicated testers as needed. This can include everything from documenting test scenarios to detailing user workflow steps to identifying the requirements for setting up user accounts, test data, and security configurations (e.g. permissions settings) in the test environment. The assistance from the Agile business analyst can (and should) also include identifying *potentially risky* functional areas in the solution that may require extra focus in the testing.

Where the Agile team only has part-time access to testers, the role of Agile business analysts in developing test cases and test plans is likely to be more substantial, preparing testing materials based on their day-to-day work with the Agile team, as well as their hands-on work with the business users. Where needed, Agile business analysts can use their intimate knowledge of the user requirements, as well as their strong familiarity with the developed software, to provide the testing team with a *comprehensive* set of test scenarios and detailed test cases, supporting test data, validation rules, and test environment configuration specifications.

The preparation of test materials is only one of the advantages of having an Agile business analyst who is a full-time member of the Agile team providing ongoing test support (versus only having intermittent testing support from part-time testers who are not co-located with the team). Further advantages are possible in the *execution* of the test cases and scenarios, as detailed in the following section.

22. Executing system and integration tests

An Agile business analyst who is an active part of the Agile team can become an indispensable resource when it comes to quality assurance and testing while the development work is being undertaken. While the Agile developers are performing unit testing, the Agile business analyst can be undertaking ongoing system, integration, data, security, and performance testing; and, where needed, assisting the developers in investigating identified bugs.

Even in a continuous integration environment with an automated testing harness, the Agile business analyst can be performing quality checks that cannot be easily captured by automated tests, including usability testing, confirming screen layouts and language, testing of online help instructions, and accessibility testing.

In addition, the Agile business analyst can be preparing the test data and test environment for the execution of the full suite of test cases by the testing team.

As the team gets closer to the end of each iteration, the involvement of the Agile business analyst in the testing work is likely to intensify, particularly where issues are identified that need to be addressed before the developed functionality is presented to the business users.

Interestingly, this is the time when the testing role of the Agile business analyst may be more important than assisting in the execution of test cases concurrent to development work. Their direct involvement with the business users, and the trusted relationship that is likely to result between them, means the Agile business analyst is often able to help the Agile developers to negotiate the *most appropriate action* to undertake when a usability or functional issue is found in the business users' testing.

This is a substantial digression from Agile approaches where the business users are only available at the end of an iteration. With limited access to the business users during the iteration, the Agile developers often need to make assumptions on behalf of the business user as to whether an error found is an 'acceptable' issue in the system, that is:

- whether the business users would consider the issue found to be a showstopper that needs to be fixed before the software can be released
- whether the business users would be happy for the issue to be released into the live environment, but logged as a known issue (and recorded in the backlog, if needed, for future action)
- whether there are viable functional alternatives and/or business process workarounds that the business users would be willing to implement in lieu of the originally requested functionality.

This is particularly important where the issue found is not easily fixed, and substantial further development work would be required. In these situations, the Agile business analyst may be able to persuade the business users to identify viable temporary or long-term workarounds to bypass the need for a development fix.

23. Executing preliminary acceptance tests

Acceptance testing is one more critical testing area where the Agile business analyst can provide value to the Agile team. For most projects, it is the responsibility of the business users to run acceptance tests to confirm the capabilities of developed software (and, where needed, provide formal sign-off) before the functionality is released into the live environment. Where a business user has limited time or availability to undertake these tests, the Agile business analyst can perform preliminary acceptance tests on their behalf and advise them of the testing results. This preliminary testing can be undertaken at any point in the iteration where the Agile developers are satisfied the software is working as agreed. The initial acceptance testing results provided by the Agile business analyst can assist the Agile developers in identifying and addressing issues that, under normal circumstances, would not have been apparent until the walkthrough session at the end of the iteration. Depending on the length of the iteration, and the timing of software availability for testing, this can give the Agile developers several weeks of advanced notice of potential issues. It can also assist in work planning for the next iteration, as critical issues would be logged alongside other prioritized capabilities for development.

This assistance from the Agile business analyst does not negate the need for the business users to conduct their own acceptance testing before giving their approval. It does, however, provide the business users with an opportunity to get initial results that can help to guide the areas of the system they focus on more stringently when they are available to perform the acceptance testing themselves. It can also provide the business users with an existing testing structure and detailed test cases they can opt to use in their own acceptance testing activities.

24. Advising on training requirements

Part of the planning for software development inevitably includes discussion on what will be required to support the solution in the live environment, including user documentation, system documentation, and, for most systems, some level of user training. The hands-on work the Agile business analyst does with the business users is likely to include initial discussions on identifying who the target audiences for the system are, and what level of formal training each audience would require beyond the support that may be provided in the documentation.

At the beginning of the project, much of the identification of training requirements is speculative, reasonable 'best guesses' on how complicated the developed solution will be, and how easily users will be able to incorporate it into their day-to-day operations. As software development progresses, and more information is known about system design and behavior, these originally speculated training requirements will need to be refined to reflect the actual capabilities of the developed system. With Agile approaches, the ongoing availability of *fully functional* software provides the organization with an even greater opportunity for system usability (and subsequent training needs) to be identified and accommodated earlier in the project. The involvement of the Agile business analyst in the identification of requirements, and in the ongoing testing of the software, allows the business users and the Agile development team to specifically identify the areas of the system that are likely to be the least intuitive for users and, therefore, require the greatest amount of training and support.

When Agile business analysts are involved in testing the solution, this can also provide them with a greater understanding of system behavior, including the areas of the system that may be more difficult for users to understand. The Agile business analysts have the added benefit of knowing the requirements identified by the business users firsthand, as well as an awareness of the underlying business processes and drivers that the developed software is intended to support. This enables the Agile business analysts to feed any usability concerns back to the business users during the development process, giving the business area advanced notice of additional (or reduced) training needs once the system goes live. This direct familiarity with the solution also allows the Agile business analysts to identify extra training that may be required for new hires (who would not have received the original training support) and for intermittent users (who may have been trained months before they are required to use the software). It can also assist in the identification of alternative training options (e.g. computer-based training modules) that may be needed, particularly where the user base is distributed across multiple offices.

As with acceptance testing, the involvement of the Agile business analyst does not negate the need for the business users to make their own assessments of training requirements once the developed software is available for review. It does, however, provide another opportunity for the organization to better prepare itself by knowing the actual training requirements in advance, which can help to minimize delays in implementation and rollout.

25. Providing training services

As Agile business analysts are familiar with both the software solution and the target users, this creates an ideal opportunity to get their assistance in creating audience-driven training materials, designing training coursework, and, where needed, conducting training classes.

In particular, the Agile business analyst is in a position to develop interactive training materials with *relevant* examples that reflect the real-world situations these users encounter in their day-to-day work. This can make the training courses much more compelling for the attendees, as well as:

- increasing their retention rates
- improving their ability to directly apply what they have learned from the training course in their ongoing operational activities.

Where training is conducted online, for example, through computer-based training, the Agile business analyst is likely to be sufficiently skilled to not only provide the content of the coursework materials but also to physically create (and maintain) the training modules on behalf of the team. Depending on the structure of the online training, the Agile business analyst may also be able to provide participants with hands-on support during the online training through chat sessions, remote screen sharing, etc.

Being the training instructor (either in the classroom or online) also gives the Agile business analyst firsthand awareness of the concerns expressed by users – and any confusion they have in using the software – which can greatly assist the Agile team in structuring the most effective user documentation for post-training user support.

It can also provide input into ongoing requirements identification, solution design, and acceptance testing activities, giving both the business users and the Agile development team additional practical user scenarios that reflect how the solution is likely to be used by each audience.

The value of the Agile business analyst in solution training is not restricted to their direct involvement in preparing or conducting training courses. Even where the Agile team has access to professional trainers who prepare the coursework materials and lead the classes, the Agile business analyst can assist these trainers by providing real-life business input into their training scenarios, trailing/testing their materials, and, where appropriate, acting as assistants to work hands-on with attendees during the training course itself.

26. Writing content for online help screens

The development of required solution documentation was previously identified as an activity the Agile business analyst is able to do on behalf of the Agile team throughout the project timeline, particularly where the team does not have access to professional technical writers who are available to assist in this work. Where the Agile business analyst who is involved in developing the solution documentation is also involved in testing the software and assisting in training, there is an ideal opportunity to combine all of these activities in the development of highly relevant content for the online help screens delivered with the solution. This is not only a practical use of the Agile business analyst in reducing the amount of work the Agile developers need to deliver, it can actually be a *more practical* approach than enlisting the assistance of a professional technical writer to do this work.

There is a tendency for technical writers who are not intimately familiar with the software – or with the users – to develop 'verbatim' support materials, for example, screenshots that literally describe the name and function of each field without giving the users the business context of *how* each field should be used in their daily work. This is often what occurs when technical writers are only brought in to assist at specific points in the project, as opposed to being an integrated member of the development team.

Agile business analysts are not only familiar with the operational activities of the users – as well as the business users' vision for the solution - they are often just as familiar with the functionality of the developed software. If you combine this with:

- the detailed knowledge of system behavior the Agile business analysts acquired from their testing work;
- the direct awareness of the users' perspectives (and issues) they gained from their involvement in the training activities;

this puts the Agile business analyst in a unique position to develop online help materials that are both technically accurate and truly meaningful to the target users.

Depending on the design of the solution, it may also be possible for the Agile business analyst to produce the online help content themselves, with minimal assistance (and time) required from the Agile developers (similar to the approach identified for computer-based training materials). This can provide substantial time savings for the developers, both in the initial production of the online help content and in the ongoing refinement of the content as the solution matures.

27. Preparing release notes and known issues lists

The implementation and release of the solution (or selected parts of the solution) into a live environment generally requires the Agile team to provide the target users with:

- release notes (to identify what capabilities are included in this release of the software, as well as any previously reported bugs that have been fixed)
- a known issues list (to detail any known technical or usability issues in the released software and, where appropriate, provide recommended workarounds).

The preparation of these materials is generally done as late as possible before the scheduled software release, in order for these documents to reflect the most current information available about the system. Ironically, this is one of the few areas in which traditional waterfall approaches have an advantage over Agile approaches. When the project team is using a traditional waterfall approach, although there is limited time for creating these materials, the team has the 'luxury' of reasonably knowing the scope and capabilities of the scheduled software release well in advance of the live migration (as the development work will have been frozen weeks – and sometimes months – in advance of the release). For project teams using Agile approaches, however, the ongoing development work undertaken throughout each iteration means there can be additions and modifications to the delivered solution much closer to the scheduled release date. Although the updates that occur closer to the live delivery date are generally not substantial changes to the system (unless a significant bug or infrastructure issue is found at the last minute), the release notes and known issues list in an Agile project need to be continually treated as a 'work in progress' until the software for delivery in the live release is finalized.

When the Agile development team is responsible for preparing these materials at the end of the iteration, this time limitation can add substantial pressure to the developers, particularly when they are also involved in setting up the live environment (e.g. migrating snapshots of the most current data from legacy systems, configuring user accounts) at the same time. The more the Agile business analyst can do to offload this work from them, and to free them to prepare for the live release, the more focused they can be on ensuring the solution itself is delivered correctly.

This is not to say the production of release notes and known issues lists cannot be undertaken to some extent *concurrent to the development work*, using the agreed subset of capabilities for the iteration(s) as a guideline. If team resources are available to compile this list as the development (and testing) work is progressing, this can alleviate some of the pressure closer to the release date. There will still be a need to confirm and refine these materials based on the final software package for delivery, but the time required for this – and the associated pressure – can be substantially reduced if advanced work has been done.

It is worth noting there is a difference between release notes that provide short descriptions of each delivered function in the software (e.g. as lines in a spreadsheet), and release notes that provide the target users with contextual information about how each included function impacts their operational activities.

Most software developers tend to think of release notes as a *laundry list* of the delivered capabilities in the software, advising the business of the scope of functions included in that release. Some development teams actually structure their release notes by listing each module, component, or even filename that is included in the migration package, with a brief note next to each, describing what function it addresses. Although this allows the release notes to be used as a checklist to identify released capabilities at a high level – and confirm implementation work – it does little to help the users of the solution to understand how these additions and updates will affect their work.

Even the best Agile developers are not immune to providing insufficient details in their release notes. For them, the originally agreed list of capabilities for each iteration (e.g. the 'above the line' features in the product backlog) becomes an easy mechanism for identifying and documenting what capabilities have been included in each release. Although this information can be far more comprehensive than a list of compiled software components or filenames, it tends to describe the *business requirements for*, not the *business impacts of*, each delivered feature. For example, consider the function identified in the following user story:

As a customer-support representative, when I am on the phone with a customer, I want to be able to view a log of their previous calls so I can identify any outstanding or recurring issues.

The corresponding item in the product backlog may read 'view a log of previous customer calls' and may include some supporting details, for example, the original user story, existing customer call reports, a logged issues list for the previous month.

When the software package that includes this capability is released, the tendency will be for the Agile development team to identify 'view a log of previous customer calls' as one of the included features, with a link to the corresponding item and supporting materials in the features list. As needed, there may also be references to any identified bugs or constraints for this feature in the known issues list (e.g. 'customer call log screen cannot be resized'). Further details on this capability may be provided in the iteration review session, updates to the user guides, or in refresher training courses, but, more often than not, it is left to the users to 'play with' this capability to understand how to use it in their daily operations. If the delivered function is complicated, does not work as the users expected, or does not align to their normal work procedures, this lack of information in the release can lead to user errors, user frustration, and, ultimately, a degree of user dissatisfaction in the delivered solution.

With the assistance of an Agile business analyst, there is an opportunity to expand on the information provided in the release notes to better describe the behavior – and the constraints – of the delivered capability. At a minimum, this can include:

- Screenshots to describe the customer call log, which include demonstrating its features (e.g. re-ordering of columns, sorting).
- A description of the business rules and constraints of the customer call log, such as:
  - it will not show calls more than six months old
  - the user needs to go to a separate screen to see calls that have been escalated for management resolution

- the export feature only includes the first 500 characters of the call description.

- Recommended workarounds for identified constraints, for example, if you need to see calls that are more than six months old, you will need to go to the reports module and run a detailed profile report for that customer.

Including this additional information in the release notes saves the user from having to separately search for each new feature in the user manuals, or to recall the walkthrough of each new feature in the iteration review session, training courses, etc.

The Agile business analyst has the business knowledge (and often more time than the developers) to provide users with these enhanced release notes that can genuinely assist them in practically applying the capabilities of the delivered solution in their day-to-day work.

28. Assisting in cross-organizational communication

The point raised in the previous section is an important one: in many cases, the work undertaken by the Agile development team is not only a mechanism for delivering a required software solution; it is a 'proof of concept' of whether Agile approaches are right for the organization. An Agile project that is successfully delivered – on time, within budget, with relevant, high-quality functionality and satisfied users – is likely to inspire other project teams and to gain management support in the use of Agile methods for future projects. Equally, an Agile project that fails in one or more of these measures may provide the opportunity for critics (and risk-averse managers) to use this project as a perpetual excuse to stick with traditional waterfall approaches. This puts a lot of pressure on the project deliverables (and on the Agile team) to ensure the organization is well positioned to receive the delivered solution. The starting point for getting corporate awareness and support is generally through ongoing *cross-organizational communication* about the solution – and about the Agile process – well before the system is released into a live environment.

Engaging in cross-organizational communication is more than simply a public relations exercise aimed at making people in the organization aware that the project is taking place. Effective communication provides an opportunity to:

- emphasize how the solution will benefit the business areas and the organization overall
- set expectations on what the solution will – and will not – deliver
- create a groundswell of support that encourages people to become more involved in the project
- get management awareness of the importance of the project to ensure ongoing funding and availability of the required resources.

The very nature of Agile approaches already lays the groundwork for cross-organizational communication through the business users who are directly involved in the project, as well as any additional stakeholders who will have been consulted throughout the process.

The Agile business analyst can supplement these communications by:

- creating content about the solution for the corporate intranet, including progress reports and, where appropriate, videos of the capabilities that have already been developed

- conducting demonstrations of developed capabilities at internal meetings, including meetings specifically scheduled for this purpose
- engaging in – and encouraging other Agile team members to engage in – casual discussion about the project with co-workers around the office.

This last bullet point is an important one. Every member of the Agile team should be an *active champion* of the solution. The Agile business analyst can provide the materials and the mechanisms for getting more corporate awareness of the solution the Agile team is developing, but it is the responsibility of everyone on the Agile team to find opportunities to spread the word in the lunchroom, after hours get-togethers, department meetings – even the proverbial water cooler (which, for most software developers, is likely to be the soda machine!) Any opportunity to increase awareness and support is likely to benefit the project team, as shown in the following section.

29. Acquiring additional and ongoing project funding

The software solution the Agile team is developing is likely to be one of many concurrent initiatives the organization is undertaking, most of which are competing for the same limited resources and budget. Although Agile methods are positioned to deliver more visible results to the organization than traditional project approaches, there are no guarantees other areas of the organization are not on the lookout for a greater portion of the available budget (or to reallocate Agile team members for other work). This is particularly true when the other initiatives being undertaken are using traditional waterfall approaches, as these projects are likely to be perpetually over-budget and constantly in need of additional funds and staff.

The cross-organizational communication described in the previous section provides a strong mechanism for ensuring the Agile solution stays prominent in people's minds, especially in the minds of the decision makers who hold the corporate purse strings. The organization-wide awareness of the Agile solution – and the benefits it is positioned to give the organization – makes it much more difficult for management to quietly stop, postpone, or even downsize the Agile project. There can still be a risk, however, when the benefits of the Agile solution are more generalized (e.g. 'will provide better phone support to customers') and not based in measurable net gains for the organization (e.g. 'will reduce the operating costs of the call center by 12 percent').

The Agile business analyst can provide the Agile team with an opportunity to put forward a *stronger business case* for the solution than generalized or anecdotal evidence can support. This includes *quantifying* the benefits the Agile solution is expected to deliver for the organization as:

- volume of increased sales
- percentage reductions in staff time
- percentage (or volume) of increases in productivity
- cost reductions in staff training (and re-training)
- percentage of fewer defects.

This enables management to assign a *bottom-line dollar figure* to the value of the project.

These figures can be supported by the *expected business value* and *business-value return* calculations that were done in support of prioritizing the feature list (see *Assessing the business value and priority of each capability* earlier in this section for further detail).

Where the Agile project is expected to deliver significant *qualitative benefits*, such as better customer service or increased employee satisfaction, these benefits can be harder to present as a compelling business case, unless they can be quantified through measurement, for example, satisfaction surveys. That is not to say these benefits are not equally important to the organization; simply that they will not resonate in the minds of the decision makers in the same way quantifiable profits and overhead cost savings will.

The business case developed by the Agile business analyst can be used for:

- securing *ongoing funding* for an Agile project that is currently underway
- positioning the Agile team to get funding for *future iterations*, where additional high business-value capabilities have been identified by the business users
- encouraging the organization to invest in other Agile projects, including the staff education needed to support these projects.

The more compelling a business case the Agile business analyst can put together on behalf of the Agile team, the more secure the current – and future – Agile project work will be. For an organization with limited funds to waste on traditional waterfall projects, this could be the *second most important* activity the Agile business analyst can undertake in support of the Agile team. The *most important* activity is the one described in the following section.

30. Providing business continuity for the Agile developers

As described in *Chapter 4: What are the Risks of Not Having an Agile Business Analyst?*, one of the biggest risks to any Agile project is the potential for the business users to be unavailable when key information and critical decisions are needed by the team. This lack of availability can put the Agile development work at a virtual (or *actual*) standstill while the team awaits further input and direction from the business areas. It can also result in the Agile developers being forced to make assumptions and decisions on behalf of the business areas, which can lead to incorrect system behavior and wasted resource time. Although the risk of wasted time is much more contained with Agile methods than with traditional waterfall approaches, it is still a risk the organization is in a position to avoid with the proper contingency planning. The containment of this risk also depends on the minimum availability of the business users at the start and end of each iteration, which may not always be possible.

Having an Agile business analyst on the project allows the Agile development team to get real-time, objective feedback on business requirements *whenever* this information is needed, even if the business users are unavailable for an extended period of time. This does not negate the need for the business users to be available for the iteration planning and review sessions, but it provides the Agile team with the ability to make well-founded solution decisions on behalf of the business users in between these sessions.

The Agile business analyst provides the Agile developers with the continuity of an *ongoing resource* who is likely to have:

- worked directly with the business users in the identification, description, valuation, and prioritization of the user stories
- interviewed the full range of stakeholders who have a vested interest in the delivered solution
- studied the existing business processes and operational procedures of the affected business areas
- researched the business constraints for the solution, including underlying policies and mandates
- worked with the testers, trainers, and technical writers to better understand the business context of each user audience
- investigated legacy systems in detail, including the system(s) the solution is intended to replace
- analyzed the data mapping, conversion, and migration requirements; interface requirements for external systems; permissions and security requirements; and capacity planning requirements for the solution.

Agile business analysts are also able to combine their detailed knowledge of the business requirements for the solution with their previous experience in requirements identification and solution design on other projects, which can give the Agile development team a reliable alternative option for getting the business feedback they need to progress their work when the business users are not available.

It is important to emphasize that the involvement of the Agile business analyst allows timely interim decisions to be made based on a reasonable level of business knowledge, with the final confirmation (and decision making) left for the business users to provide at the planning and review sessions. The Agile business analyst is not intended to be a replacement for the business users over long periods of time, as that can add greater risk that the delivered solution does not match the business users' expectations when they are finally available to undertake this review.

That being said, there may be circumstances when the business users become *completely unavailable* to assist on the project due to internal staffing changes, personal commitments, employee turnover, or urgent unplanned work (e.g. audits, disaster recovery). In these circumstances, the organization may opt to put a hold on project work until the required business representatives are available again. In some cases, replacement staff from the business areas may be available to assist the Agile development team, but they may not have the same level of detailed business knowledge as the original business users. Alternatively, the organization may determine the solution the Agile team is developing is too critical to be postponed.

Having the Agile business analyst directly involved with the business users throughout the project timeline provides the Agile development team – and the organization – with a 'safety net' if business users are no longer available to work on the project altogether. Although Agile business analysts cannot bring the breadth and depth of operational knowledge that the business users can, they can provide a reasonable understanding of the requirements from their hands-on work with the business areas. This can give the Agile development team the continuity needed to allow the project work to continue while arrangements are being made to replace the business users. It also allows for more comprehensive knowledge transfer from the Agile team to any newly assigned business users. Most importantly, having an Agile business analyst on the team means Agile development work does not need to be put on hold indefinitely.

CHAPTER 6: GETTING THE RIGHT AGILE BUSINESS ANALYST FOR YOUR TEAM

The previous chapter identified 30 core activities that an Agile business analyst can undertake to assist the project team in making the delivered solution as valuable as possible.

The following chapters provide guidelines for progressing your pursuit of the highest business-value solution in your Agile work, starting with what you can do to ensure that you get the most capable and valuable Agile business analyst for the particular needs of your team (*Chapter 6: Getting the Right Agile Business Analyst for your Team*); followed by what activities the Agile business analyst can do to best support the current and future work of your team (*Chapter 7: Moving Your Agile Team Forward*); and concluding with a range of general and practice-specific Agile and business analysis resources that can be used to support these activities (*Chapter 8: More Information on Agile*). The first step in moving your Agile team forward is finding the best Agile business analyst for your specific needs.

There is a significant difference between hiring an experienced business analyst and hiring a business analyst who is *truly capable* of working within an Agile environment.

Traditional training for business analysts is focused on the identification and documentation of user requirements, with a strong emphasis on the need for comprehensive and detailed specification documentation. This means business analysts who have only worked on waterfall projects in traditional IT environments would be used to creating piles of specification documentation for management sign-off, with some believing the measure of their success is in the height of the documentation pile. Regular, incremental review and adjustment of specifications is virtually unheard of on traditional waterfall projects, as it generally takes weeks (and sometimes months) to get stakeholder approval for these documents. This means that, once the requirements documentation is completed, the traditional business analyst tends to move on to another project team, only returning if there are significant changes to the initially identified system requirements or (occasionally) when the developed system is ready for testing. Instead of being an integral ongoing part of the development team, the traditional business analyst is seen to be a *temporary resource* who is no longer required once the 'requirements phase' of the project is complete.

This historical role of business analysts might scare some Agile teams into thinking it would be too difficult to break a traditional business analyst from reverting to an upfront requirements mindset, from defaulting to documentation as the primary communication tool, from seeing a frozen, signed-off system instead of an evolving solution. That is, until you consider most Agile software developers themselves started out on traditional waterfall project teams. If they could break free from the handcuffs of upfront requirements, there is no reason why a traditional business analyst *with the right mindset* could not do the same.

***Building* the ideal Agile business analyst**

Agile teams who want to include an Agile business analyst who can genuinely add value to their project team should be less focused on *finding* the right business analyst, and more focused on *building* the right one. Unless you are fortunate enough to have a business analyst who has successfully worked on a range of Agile projects, you will most likely be selecting a traditional business analyst with the right attitude, skills, and knowledge to work within an Agile environment, and then training them hands-on on Agile approaches as the project progresses. The key is in identifying the qualities that best position a traditional business analyst to successfully make this transition.

Qualifications

Although there are a handful of formal certification programs available for IT business analysts (for example, the *Certified Business Analysis Professional* and *Certification of Competency in Business Analysis* designations offered by the ***International Institute of Business Analysis***[1]), there are many business analysts who have taken on their role without any formal qualifications, except for their hands-on experience on IT projects.

In some cases, new starters would have been sent on a business analysis skills training course, but these courses are generally focused on waterfall approaches and artifacts, for example, how to create a detailed functional requirements specification, develop a traceability matrix, and build use case diagrams. Many business analysis training courses incorporate requirements identification skills, advising the business analyst on how to work with individual users and stakeholder groups, how to reconcile differences in stakeholder perspectives, and how to

1 Further details are available at iiba.org.

translate a verbal requirement into a written specification. Some courses include training on strategic and operational analysis toolsets, such as enterprise architecture frameworks, balanced scorecards, and business process modeling, in order to give the IT business analyst context on how the developed solution fits within the overall business requirements of the organization.

The more forward-thinking training courses may even identify Agile methods as one of a number of possible software development approaches, but it is reasonably rare to find a course that specifically trains business analysts on how to work in an Agile environment[2].

All of this means that assessing the suitability of a potential Agile business analyst is not as simple as looking for the right acronym on their application form (unless, of course, they have a qualification in Agile methods, such as certified Scrum product owner training[3]). Instead, you need to focus on the attitude, skills, and knowledge of each candidate.

Attitude

It is our attitude at the beginning of a difficult task which, more than anything else, will affect its successful outcome. – William James[4].

It may seem unusual to make attitude the first criterion for finding an effective Agile business analyst. Surely the

---

2 Some noted exceptions are the Agile business analyst courses offered by Learning Tree International (*www.learningtree.co.uk/courses/3511/business-analysis-in-an-agile-environment/*), Software Education (*www.softed.com.au/courses/the-agile-business-analyst.aspx*), and EBG Consulting (*http://ebgconsulting.com/agile-business-analysis.php*).

3 *http://www.scrumalliance.org/pages/certified_scrum_product_owner*.

4 Multiple sources.

experience of a prospective candidate is more important than their state of mind?

As identified in the previous section, it is reasonably rare to find a business analyst who has direct experience – or formal training – in working with Agile projects. If you are looking to include an effective Agile business analyst on your team, you are better positioned to find someone with a reasonable level of experience in undertaking business analysis tasks on traditional IT projects, but who genuinely appreciates the strength of Agile approaches and is eager to trial these approaches firsthand. This could include someone who:

- has been frustrated on a previous software development project when necessary and valuable system changes could not be implemented because the system was already signed off by management
- wishes they had the opportunity to work more directly with the business user throughout the development process, including jointly assessing software as it becomes available for hands-on review to see if it genuinely meets their needs
- is concerned when software development teams spend too much time focusing on low-value features instead of delivering the most critical capabilities in each release
- sees prototypes (even functional prototypes) as potentially dangerous because they can give business users a false impression of system behavior and stability
- understands the value of identifying and addressing risks as early as possible in the project timeline.

In short, the best Agile business analyst candidate is someone who:

- understands the weaknesses in traditional waterfall projects (e.g. upfront analysis activities, piles of documentation, separation of the development team from the business users, immutable requirements) – even someone who has been burnt by these approaches in a previous project
- appreciates the value of working collaboratively with the business users throughout the development process, working hands-on with fully functional software, focusing the team on delivering the highest business-value features (instead of the highest volume, the sexiest, or the most technically challenging ones).

There is one other determining factor for the attitude of the business analyst candidate that has been deliberately left off of the list until now:

- Someone who prefers to work hands-on with the business users than to create piles of documentation.

The reason this was not on the original list is because, deep down inside, most business analysts (dare I say all business analysts?) really dread having to write up pages and pages of functional specifications. Truly good business analysts are communicators and problem solvers who are at their best when they are working directly with stakeholders. Working hands-on with business users to assess their requirements can be challenging and exciting – even fun – especially when the business analyst is helping the users to overcome a difficult issue. Going back to an isolated desk, however, to turn piles of written notes into structured, carefully worded, numbered, and cross-referenced requirements matrices can be quite tedious for a business analyst, but it is a 'necessary evil' on a traditional waterfall software development project.

This is why asking a prospective Agile business analyst what they think about working directly with business users, and communicating their requirements through user stories, prioritized feature lists, and collaborative review sessions of working software – instead of writing doorstops of documentation – is a bit of a rhetorical question. That is, unless you want to use the question to weed out those candidates who prefer writing documentation to working with users!

A prospective Agile business analyst who comes to the project with contempt for the weaknesses in waterfall methodologies, and a genuine appreciation for the value in Agile approaches, is worlds apart from an 'experienced business analyst' who proudly displays the 1,200-page specification document they wrote for a previous software development project to impress you in the interview.

Skills

Having an Agile business analyst candidate with the right attitude toward Agile approaches is critical, but this mindset needs to be coupled with a strong skill set that will enable the Agile business analyst to work effectively with both the business users and the Agile development team to deliver the most valuable solution.

The core set of required skills includes:

- **Communication** – first and foremost, an Agile business analyst needs to be capable of effectively communicating with business users, development team members, management, and executives to understand their needs and to act as a liaison across all parties. The Agile business analyst should also be someone who is easy to talk to, and who makes people comfortable enough to discuss their needs and their concerns without reservation. Also, with the ever-growing number of teams distributed across multiple office locations, regions, and countries, the Agile business analyst should be capable of conducting these sessions remotely (e.g. through videoconferencing with shared browser-based screens). The Agile business analyst should also be prepared to conduct sessions through audio conference calls where required, although it may be difficult for even the most skilled Agile business analyst to achieve the desired outcomes without shared screens and some degree of face-to-face interaction.

- **Eliciting requirements** – equally important is the ability for the business analyst to be inquisitive, asking targeted questions that get to the heart of each requirement, instead of mindlessly scribing what each stakeholder says verbatim. This includes encouraging people to think beyond their 'business as usual' perspectives to see the potential benefits the right solution could bring to their area, and to the organization overall.
- **Big picture perspective** – the inquisitive nature identified in the previous bullet point is not simply a matter of having an Agile business analyst who asks questions for the sake of it. Effective Agile business analysts always have the big picture of the solution in the back of their minds – including the strategic, operational, and technical considerations – and use this context to frame the questions asked. It is the difference between asking the business user: *should the*

button say [Exit] or [Cancel]? And asking *why would a user need to cancel the process?* And *who should be authorized to cancel the process?* And *what are the implications if the process is cancelled?*

- **Attention to detail** – interestingly, the most effective business analysts are equally comfortable speaking with stakeholders at both a big-picture level and at a very detailed level, depending on what the situation requires. Interface design, validation rules, data migration and mapping, report templates, and other system specifications require the business analyst to think and communicate at a very detailed level. A theoretical business analyst who is only capable of high-level discussions – and not able to delve into the practical details of the solution – does not help the Agile development team when they are building tests, coding business rules, and designing screens.
- **Lateral thinking** – most systems are reasonably complex, covering a number of business functions and, in many cases, are built to serve a number of business areas. The Agile business analyst needs to be able to think across the traditional boundaries of dedicated roles to consider the cross-functional implications of the solution. In addition, the Agile business analyst needs to be able to assess the delivered software in conjunction with the corresponding business processes, skill sets, and resourcing levels in each area, as well as the policies and frameworks of the organization overall. The objective is to provide a holistic business solution, not a software deliverable.
- **Negotiation** – in designing and specifying a solution, it is inevitable there will be disparities between the requirements identified across stakeholders, as well as

disconnects in the discussion of those requirements with the development team. In some cases, these can be resolved with greater communication between the parties. In other cases, they represent genuinely conflicting requirements (or conflicting priorities assigned to requested features). An effective Agile business analyst is able to work with all involved parties to come to a reasonable middle ground that services the best interests of the organization overall. This is often a combination of clarification and compromise, which requires both strong diplomatic and communication skills to be achieved effectively.

- **Public speaking** – the communication skills identified in the first bullet point are not limited to one-on-one discussions with stakeholders. In many cases, the Agile business analyst will need to be able to work effectively with groups of people, both to gather their requirements and to facilitate subsequent clarification and negotiation discussions. In addition, the Agile business analyst may need to provide training services to groups of users during and after the implementation of the solution. In all of these situations, the Agile business analyst needs to be comfortable speaking in front of a roomful of people, engaging and interacting with the audience, and addressing potential conflicting perspectives in the group without getting sidetracked.
- **Flexibility** – in Agile environments, team members need to be prepared to take on any role required to progress the project. Usually, this is a short-term activity, for example, asking developers to assist in urgently testing data migrations or writing newly requested user documentation. For some projects, particularly those with small teams, the need to take on

multiple roles is an ongoing requirement to compensate for the limited availability (or skill sets) of team members. This is where Agile business analysts are especially valuable, as they can effectively serve as testers, technical writers, and trainers as the project requires. It is, however, critical the Agile business analyst be flexible enough to take on these roles, even at a moment's notice.

- **Training** – having the ability to speak comfortably in front of a group of people is a significant strength for an Agile business analyst who is taking on a training role, but it is preferable, where possible, to have an Agile business analyst who has formal experience as a software trainer (including in the development of training materials). There is an art to effectively presenting and explaining solutions in the language and context of the audience, as well as working with the audience to confirm and clarify their understanding. Experienced software trainers know how to turn a software walkthrough into an engaging and educational session for attendees. An Agile business analyst who has this experience brings yet another skill set that enhances the overall value of the Agile team.
- **Testing** – similar to the training skill identified in the previous bullet point, there is an art to effective software testing. Having an Agile business analyst on the team who is available and willing to do functional or usability testing of software in progress is valuable. Having an Agile business analyst on the team who is an experienced quality assurance specialist with formal knowledge of testing methods, test execution, and test documentation is indispensable.

- **Documentation** – last, but far from least, is the need for the Agile business analyst to produce effective written communication at all levels and to all audiences. Although Agile approaches encourage face-to-face communication in lieu of documentation wherever possible, it is a rare software project that does not require some level of project documentation, user documentation, and/or system documentation, even if this documentation is produced post-implementation. The Agile business analyst should be skilled at – and fully prepared to produce – whatever documentation is reasonably required for the project. Any prospective candidate who thinks becoming an Agile business analyst means never having to write another document is not someone you would want to include on your team.

The preceding list is, by no means, a checklist of the minimum absolute requirements for hiring an Agile business analyst who can add value to the Agile team. This list is intended to provide you with general guidelines on the range of skills a prospective Agile business analyst with the right attitude could bring. It is not realistic for you to expect every Agile business analyst candidate should – or will – have all of the capabilities previously listed. Ideally, the unique combination of these skills the candidate brings will complement the strengths and weaknesses of the existing Agile team. As the team works collaboratively, there will be greater levels of knowledge sharing and cross-training to enhance these skills for all team members, including the Agile business analyst.

Knowledge

The Agile business analyst is not – and should not claim to be – a substitute for the business expertise of the users or for the technical expertise of the Agile development team. The primary role of the Agile business analyst is *communicator* and *liaison*, bridging the gap between groups to achieve a shared understanding that reflects the expertise of each participant. It is, therefore, important the Agile business analyst has enough business and technical knowledge to genuinely understand each stakeholder, to appreciate their challenges, and to be able to see things from their perspective.

It is worthwhile noting that, in some cases, having a reasonable level of business and technical knowledge is also needed for the Agile business analyst to earn the respect and trust of stakeholders, especially those who have had bad experiences in the past working with people who did not take the time to understand their needs.

Although the Agile business analyst is not expected to have all the expertise of the stakeholders, the business analyst should be knowledgeable enough not to rely on having these resources at hand in every situation. In any project, there will be circumstances where the business analyst will not have ready access to expert resources, and will need to work independently. This is particularly true in situations where the Agile business analyst has been asked to serve as a *proxy* for the business users, generally due to lack of availability because of ongoing commitments in their primary roles (see *What to do when the business user is not available*). Although the Agile business analyst does not have the benefit of stakeholder knowledge in these situations, they should be fully prepared – and knowledgeable enough – to progress the project even when these resources are unavailable, including recording questions that arise which they are unable to address without the participation of these stakeholders.

When acting as a liaison (or even as a proxy), it is extremely important the Agile business analyst has enough self-awareness (and humility) to know the boundaries of their knowledge. Effective Agile business analysts are as comfortable in answering a question as they are in advising they do not know the answer, and then offering to investigate it further. If you are interviewing a prospective Agile business analyst candidate, you may want to deliberately include a question the candidate could not reasonably have the answer to (for example, asking about a relatively new Agile method or technique). If the prospective Agile business analyst readily admits to not knowing about the topic, but offers to research it, that is a reasonably good sign the candidate is comfortable advising people on what they do not know (i.e. they do not see the need for follow-up as a weakness). If the candidate fumbles to try to *appear* to know the answer or, even worse, confidently responds with an incorrect answer, that should trigger some alarm bells in the back of your mind about whether this candidate is the best person to work with your stakeholders.

Having emphasized the importance of the Agile business analyst seeking the expertise of business users and Agile developers, it is also critical to make the distinction between *considering* the information they provide and *deferring* to it. The Agile business analyst is responsible for both *eliciting* and *critiquing* the information these stakeholders provide. Expert resources, even the most knowledgeable ones, generally respond to questions based on their individual experiences and their familiarity with current practices and processes. An effective Agile business analyst needs to be objective and confident enough to question the information presented, yet respectful enough to do so in a way that does not offend the speaker. This delicate balance of diplomacy and determination is a skill unto itself. A prospective Agile business analyst who is able to achieve this should be seen as a strong candidate for the position.

In discussing the knowledge a prospective Agile business analyst brings to the project, it is also important to consider if they have had any exposure to (or formal training) in Agile methods. Although getting an Agile business analyst with direct experience in working on Agile projects is reasonably rare, any familiarity they have with Agile methods is a benefit, especially if this knowledge has helped them to understand and appreciate the differences between Agile and traditional waterfall approaches.

Like any new member of an Agile team, it is recommended an Agile business analyst who is not already familiar with Agile approaches should endeavor to read introductory resources on Agile (see *Chapter 8: More Information on Agile*) and, where possible, attend an on-site or online training course. This basic understanding of the core principles and practices of Agile approaches includes:

- why solutions are *emergent* and not predefined
- why the business user is involved throughout the process
- why the team is deliberately *self-managing* and *cross-disciplinary*
- why it is important to deliver *fully functional capabilities* instead of screen mock-ups.

Without this understanding, much of the value of having an Agile business analyst on the team is likely to be lost.

If you are a traditional business analyst…

If you are a business analyst who has worked on traditional waterfall software development projects, and you want to start working on an Agile software development team, then everything covered in this chapter applies to you, only in reverse. Instead of being the IT manager who wants to find the right Agile business analyst to build the best possible Agile team, you are looking to be the *strongest candidate* for that team. This means that you need to bring the right combination of attitude, skills, and knowledge to complement the other team members on the project, noting that attitude, more than anything, could be the deciding factor.

Before you interview for the position, it is strongly recommended that you take the time to familiarize yourself with Agile principles and methods (see *Chapter 8: More Information on Agile* for a list of resources that can assist in your education). This is not only to impress the interviewer with your extensive knowledge of Agile approaches but also to confirm whether you are truly comfortable working in an environment with evolving requirements, time-based deliverables, and ongoing demands for testing, training, and documentation.

It would also be valuable for you to assess yourself and your experience against the *skills* list provided previously. Although you may not have worked directly on Agile projects, you might be able to show your capabilities (e.g. communication, negotiation, training) from the other projects you have worked on, even if they used waterfall methods.

Most importantly, you need to be able to identify and articulate *why* you want to work on Agile projects, particularly in comparison to waterfall methods. This will demonstrate to the interviewer that you have a genuine appreciation for the strengths of Agile approaches, and the right attitude to deliver a successful outcome.

The bottom line

As noted in the *skills* section, it is not realistic for an interviewer to expect every prospective Agile business analyst will have the full scope of capabilities listed previously. Building the ideal Agile business analyst is really a matter of finding a candidate with the right combination of attitude, skills, knowledge, and *potential* to fit in with the dynamic of your Agile team. It is the hands-on work with the Agile team that will truly demonstrate whether the Agile business analyst can work in an evolving, collaborative, self-managing environment, and whether the team is able to make the best use of that role.

It should also be noted that the inclusion of a former traditional business analyst can come with its own challenges. One of the very common issues that can occur is the potential for business analysts who have worked primarily on waterfall projects to add a degree of 'analysis paralysis' to the requirements gathering and software review process, that is, the tendency for them to over-analyze the situation, to want to undertake further investigation before making a decision, to focus on the complex exception cases instead of the core capabilities. The iterative and adaptive nature of Agile approaches can help to encourage the newly Agile business analyst to go forward with *reasonably correct* decisions, knowing there will be an opportunity to revisit and adjust these decisions if needed as the project progresses. This assurance often allows these business analysts to 'break free' from the waterfall chains that bind them; however, as they are analysts by nature, they may occasionally need gentle reminding from the other Agile team members to refocus their thinking.

Once you have found the right candidate, the next step is deciding how to best leverage their strengths to progress the project. Ideally, this would be left to the self-managing Agile team to decide, but those Agile team members who have not actively worked with an Agile business analyst in the past may need a bit of encouragement to find the best opportunities.

CHAPTER 7: MOVING YOUR AGILE TEAM FORWARD

If the previous chapters have persuaded you to include an Agile business analyst on your project team, the next step to consider is how to best incorporate the Agile business analyst into your current and future project work. This decision should be based upon *where you are in the project timeline* and *what specific challenges* the Agile development team is facing. Key factors to consider are:

- **Project timing**: is the project:
    - at the beginning stages (requirements identification)?
    - well underway (ongoing iterative development, review, and release)?
    - at the closing stages (live release of the full solution, user training, post-implementation support)?
- **Business user availability**: does the team have access to knowledgeable business users throughout the project timeline? How available are they to assist the team? (e.g. Only at iteration planning and review sessions? 'On call' whenever the developers have questions? Full-time members of the Agile team?)
- **Highest-priority capabilities**: on what basis did the business users assign priorities to the items on the feature list? Are the highest-priority items on the feature list really the ones that will deliver the greatest business-value return to the organization (i.e. make the Agile solution as valuable as possible)? Are the business users able to *objectively* consider and prioritize the requirements of all affected stakeholders? Have alternative options (e.g. business process

improvements, policy changes) been considered, particularly where a requested capability is extremely complex – or costly – for the Agile team to develop?

- **System integration and acceptance testing**: to what extent does the team have access to system and integration testers (e.g. dedicated team members, 'on demand' resources)? Are the business users undertaking formal acceptance testing of the solution prior to live release? Who is writing the test cases, setting up the test environments, and documenting the test results?
- **Project documentation:** what organizational, project management, quality management, user support, and system administration documentation does the team need to produce? Is there a technical writer and/or a project administrator available to produce and manage these documents?
- **User training:** is there a need to formally train some (or all) of the intended users? Will training classes be held and/or online training courses be produced? Who is developing the training materials?
- **Legacy systems and data:** does the team know the capabilities, business rules, and constraints of related legacy systems? Has the legacy data needed for the solution been analyzed, mapped, cleansed, migrated, and tested?
- **Integration with external systems:** has the team analyzed what data and/or functional integration is needed from external systems? Have they identified the interchange fields and formats, validation rules, communication protocols, encryption algorithms, and scheduling parameters? Have they coordinated these

activities with the resources who are managing the external system(s)?

- **Permissions, security, and capacity requirements:** have the permissions and security requirements (including data security) been identified and confirmed? Has an assessment been made of the short-, medium-, and long-term capacity requirements for the solution, including expected storage, numbers of users, volume of transactions, and network capacity?
- **Other issues:** what other challenges are facing the team in the identification, development, testing, and delivery of the solution? Are these challenges able to be resolved with input (and decisions) from the business users, or do they require:
  - the availability of other skilled staff (e.g. database administrators, security specialists)?
  - additional project funding?
  - the acquisition of new equipment or software?
  - adherence to (or approval to bypass) corporate policies and/or external mandates?

The following list of activities is intended to provide *reasonable starting points* for where the Agile business analyst can provide the most value to your team, depending on where the solution is in the project timeline, and what specific challenges the team is facing. It is left to each team to determine – and, where needed, to *reassess* – those Agile business analyst activities that are most urgently needed at each stage of your project.

Where are you in the project timeline?

Asking an Agile team whether they are at the start, middle, or end of solution delivery may be somewhat of a loaded question. The iterative nature of Agile approaches means, in many respects, there is an *artificial boundary* that distinguishes the activities that occur at the start, middle, and end of a project. In effect, each iteration in an Agile project can incorporate *all* the activities of the software development lifecycle. So why would the activities undertaken by the Agile business analyst – and the value they add to the solution – be dependent upon how far along the Agile team is in delivering the solution?

For the purposes of this section, the distinction is being made between those activities that occur *to a more substantial degree* at the beginning of a project (e.g. scoping the entire solution) and at the end of a project (e.g. full rollout, production support, and training of system users) from the *ongoing* requirements identification, development, testing, and rollout activities that can be part of any iteration.

Although the activities undertaken by Agile business analysts can add value to the solution at any point in the project, the degree of value these activities provide will vary, depending on how much work (and time) has already been invested in the solution. For example, having the Agile business analyst work with the business users in assigning 'expected business values' for requested capabilities (and in calculating the corresponding 'business-value returns') is a much more valuable activity when it is done as part of the *initial development of the feature list* (or in one of the earlier iterations). Finding out at the end of an Agile project that the features that were included in the developed solution are not, in fact, the highest-priority capabilities required by the business areas does the organization little good in recovering expended project costs and resources. This would be similar to the Agile team *retrospectively* discovering a complex system function that was built (and rebuilt) by the developers over several iterations was for a user requirement that could – and should – have been more effectively addressed through business process changes. The earlier in the project timeline the business users are paired with Agile business analysts, and their stated solution requirements are reviewed objectively, the more likely that the Agile developers will be working with the highest-priority feature list throughout the project.

The opposite is true when an Agile business analyst is asked to undertake activities *too early* in the project timeline. For example, asking the Agile business analyst to prepare training materials, end-user documentation, or (to some extent) detailed acceptance test cases before the screen flows and user interfaces for the solution are reasonably agreed with the business users. The Agile business analyst can do some preliminary work in these areas, such as:

- creating document templates, for example, test case matrices, user guides, training workbooks
- using the *conditions of satisfaction* identified for each user story as the basis for acceptance tests
- reviewing any existing standardized materials in the organization the team deliverables need to comply with, for example, training tools.

This preliminary work can save the Agile team some time when the project gets closer to a software release, but, if it is taken too far, it could also result in more 'throw away' work than value-added work.

Another variable is the emergence of unexpected hurdles and challenges. Although these issues can occur at any point in the project timeline, they are generally easier to identify (and to resolve) when analysis work is undertaken at *the beginning of the project*, targeting those areas likely to cause the greatest risk (further detail is provided in the *What are the most likely challenges?* section that follows).

The bottom line is that identifying the most valuable activities for an Agile business analyst to undertake at any project stage is always going to be more of a generalization than a set of 'hard and fast' rules. Accordingly, the lists below are overall guidelines for you to best apply to the specific circumstances (and challenges) of your project.

At the start of the project

If you are at the beginning of your Agile project, and the business users are in the process of assessing, detailing, and prioritizing the scope of requested capabilities for the solution, the Agile business analyst is in a position to add more substantial value by undertaking the following subset of activities from *Chapter 5: 30 Ways for the Agile Business Analyst to Add Value to Your Project:*

- Identifying and confirming user stories.
- Assessing the business value and priority of each capability.
- Finding viable alternatives to satisfy business requirements.
- Complying with regulations and other mandates.
- Adhering to corporate policies.
- Reviewing and refining existing business processes.
- Getting input from all relevant stakeholders.
- Managing feature lists and priorities.
- Providing input to Agile team estimation and planning.
- Researching and resolving outstanding issues.

- Analyzing data mapping, conversion, and migration requirements.
- Analyzing interface requirements for external systems.
- Investigating legacy systems.
- Identifying permissions and security requirements.
- Advising on capacity planning.
- Assisting in asset and infrastructure acquisition.
- Developing requirements, user, or system documentation.
- Assisting in project management reporting.
- Ensuring compliance with quality management systems.
- Advising on training requirements.
- Assisting in cross-organizational communication.
- Acquiring additional and ongoing project funding.
- Providing business continuity for the Agile developers.

In the middle of the project

If you have already begun your Agile project, the requested capabilities of the solution have been identified (and refined), prioritized (and re-prioritized) – and, ideally, a portion of the development work is already underway – the Agile business analyst can best assist the Agile team by undertaking the following activities. Note the following requirements analysis activities relate to *any additional or changed functionality* from the original scope:

- Identifying and confirming user stories.
- Assessing the business value and priority of each capability.
- Finding viable alternatives to satisfy business requirements.
- Complying with regulations and other mandates.
- Adhering to corporate policies.

- Reviewing and refining existing business processes.
- Getting input from all relevant stakeholders.
- Managing feature lists and priorities.
- Providing input to Agile team estimation and planning.
- Researching and resolving outstanding issues.
- Assisting Agile team members in designing user interfaces.
- Assisting in asset and infrastructure acquisition.
- Developing requirements, user, or system documentation.
- Assisting in project management reporting.
- Ensuring compliance with quality management systems.
- Documenting test plans and test cases.
- Executing system and integration tests.
- Executing preliminary acceptance tests.
- Advising on training requirements.
- Providing training services.
- Writing content for online help screens.
- Preparing release notes and known issues lists.
- Assisting in cross-organizational communication.
- Acquiring additional and ongoing project funding.
- Providing business continuity for the Agile developers.

At the end of the project

If you are at the end of your Agile project, and in the process of implementing the developed solution, the Agile business analyst can position the organization for getting the most value from the delivered solution by undertaking the following activities:

- Researching and resolving outstanding issues.

- Assisting in asset and infrastructure acquisition.
- Developing requirements, user, or system documentation.
- Assisting in project management reporting.
- Ensuring compliance with quality management systems.
- Documenting test plans and test cases.
- Executing system and integration tests.
- Executing preliminary acceptance tests.
- Advising on training requirements.
- Providing training services.
- Writing content for online help screens.
- Preparing release notes and known issues lists.
- Assisting in cross-organizational communication.
- Acquiring additional and ongoing project funding.
- Providing business continuity for the Agile developers.

What are the most likely challenges?

As each Agile project is different in its required capabilities, system environments, and constraints, so too are the challenges each Agile team is likely to face during the course of the project. By their very nature, Agile approaches are designed around the expectation of *change*, including changes to user requirements, resources, internal and external business drivers, and underlying technologies. This flexibility can, to some extent, insulate the project (and the project team) from the normal challenges that would occur in any software development project having significant (or catastrophic) consequences on the team's ability to deliver the required solution. Even with the project's ability to accommodate change – and the Agile team's understanding that unexpected events will occur –

there is a difference between waiting for inevitable project challenges, and taking *active steps* to mitigate the likelihood (and the impact) of these events.

Several of the Agile business analyst activities described in *Chapter 5: 30 Ways for the Agile Business Analyst to Add Value to Your Project* are deliberately intended for the Agile team to investigate possible risk areas as early in the project timeline as possible.

In some cases, the investigation the Agile business analyst undertakes will result in outcomes the Agile team is already aware of (i.e. it is simply a confirmation of their understanding). One example of this might be the Agile business analyst's investigation into the structure and quality of data in legacy systems resulting in the identification of missing data in the source system, including a small number of corrupted and incomplete database records, most of which was already known to the Agile development team. In this case, all the Agile business analyst may have been able to add to the known issues was further detail about the specific database fields and records that would need to be addressed in the data migration.

In other cases, however, there is a reasonable possibility the Agile business analyst's investigation of the legacy systems will result in the identification of *substantial issues* with the database, for example, database views that will need to be created to address the complex table structures and encrypted values in the backend of the legacy system. Where a body of work is required – particularly where the resources who need to undertake this work are outside of the Agile team – the advanced notice the Agile business analyst's investigation has provided can position the team to face significantly fewer system issues and time delays down the track.

Of the 30 Agile business analyst activities identified, the ones most likely to identify the *technical* risks the Agile team can address early on are:

- Analyzing data mapping, conversion, and migration requirements
- Analyzing interface requirements for external systems
- Investigating legacy systems
- Identifying permissions and security requirements
- Advising on capacity planning.

Equally, the ones most likely to identify the *business* risks the business users (and, to some extent, the Agile team) can address early on are:

- Assessing the business value and priority of each capability
- Complying with regulations and other mandates
- Adhering to corporate policies
- Getting input from all relevant stakeholders
- Assisting in asset and infrastructure acquisition
- Assisting in cross-organizational communication
- Acquiring additional and ongoing project funding
- Providing business continuity for the Agile developers.

Not all of the risks will apply equally – if at all – to the Agile project your team is working on. Where there is the potential for any one of these risks to occur, it is valuable for the Agile team to make investigation and issue resolution a top priority for the Agile business analyst. In the best of worlds, the investigation work done by the Agile business analyst will confirm that the risk is being adequately managed and controlled by the activities the Agile team is already doing. In the worst-case scenario, the risk has been identified well in advance of when it would have inevitably occurred in the project timeline, and the Agile team is better prepared to address it or, ideally, avoid it altogether.

It should be noted that the investigation work done by the Agile business analyst may need to be revisited and, if needed, repeated as the project evolves. External systems, databases, network environments, and other solution elements are likely to be changing *concurrent* to the Agile development work. This means a risk that did not exist (or was not significant) in the initial investigation may emerge as a critical issue farther down the track. This is particularly true as each iteration identifies new priorities and capabilities the solution needs to deliver, each of which may put different demands on the infrastructure and integration requirements.

What are the natural strengths of the Agile team members?

The involvement of an Agile business analyst does not preclude the equivalent work being done by the other members of the team. Where Agile developers have a natural inclination and strength in analyzing business user requirements, these skills should be encouraged and fostered by the team. In fact, it is *strongly preferred* that these activities be undertaken by as many Agile team members as possible, to allow for knowledge-sharing and resourcing, as well as giving them a better perspective of the business users' requirements.

It is important to remember that the specific activities undertaken by the Agile business analyst should also be dependent on the strengths of the selected resource, including those skills identified in *Chapter 6: Getting the Right Agile Business Analyst for Your Team*, such as:

- communication
- eliciting requirements
- big picture perspective
- attention to detail
- lateral thinking
- negotiation
- public speaking
- flexibility
- training
- testing
- documentation.

The role of the Agile business analyst will be different for each project, and this role is likely to change as new challenges are encountered. This is why the Agile team should not only identify reasonable *starting points* where the Agile business analyst can assist but be equally open to considering *emerging* needs and opportunities as the project progresses. This will enable the Agile business analyst to provide both immediate – and ongoing – value to the team.

CHAPTER 8: MORE INFORMATION ON AGILE

The following are general, methodology-specific, and practice-specific Agile sources you can refer to for further information:

General information on Agile

- Agile alliance: *www.Agilealliance.com*
- *Agile: An Executive Guide – Real Results from IT Budgets,* Jamie Lynn Cooke, IT Governance Publishing (2011): *www.itgovernanceusa.com/shop/p-351-Agile-an-executive-guide.aspx#.uc7geqwlfg0*
- Agile Journal: *www.agilejournal.com*
- AgileKiwi – Practical Agile software development: *www.agilekiwi.com*
- Agile Manifesto: *www.agilemanifesto.org*
- *www.agilesoftwaredevelopment.com*
- Alistair Cockburn: *http://alistair.cockburn.us/*
- *Fundamentals of Agile Project Management: An Overview (Technical Manager's Survival Guides),* Gonçalves M, Heda R, Asme Press (2010): *www.amazon.com/fundamentals-Agile-project-management-technical/dp/0791802965/ref=sr_1_117?s=books&ie=utf8&qid=1297939406&sr=1-117*

- *Everything You Want to Know About Agile,* Jamie Lynn Cooke, IT Governance Publishing (2012): *www.itgovernanceusa.com/shop/p-549-everything-you-want-to-know-about-Agile.aspx#.uc7ggqwlfg0*
- The New Methodology:

  www.thoughtworks.com/articles/new-methodology

Specific Agile methodologies

Overview

- *A Practical Guide to Seven Agile Methodologies*, Coffin R, Lane D: Part One: *www.devx.com/architect/article/32761*;
  Part Two: *www.devx.com/architect/article/32836*

Scrum

- Scrum alliance: *www.scrumalliance.org*
- *Glossary of Scrum Terms,* Szalvay V, Scrum Alliance, Inc. (2007): *www.scrumalliance.org/articles/39-glossary-of-scrum-terms*
- Scrum and Agile presentations by Mike Cohn of Mountain Goat Software (various dates): *www.mountaingoatsoftware.com/presentations*

DSDM

- *What is DSDM?* Clifton M, Dunlap J (2003): *www.codeproject.com/kb/architecture/dsdm.aspx*
- *DSDM Explained*, Davies R, Jaoo (2004): *www.agilexp.com/presentations/dsdmexplained.pdf*

FDD™

- *An Overview of FDD™ – Web Development Methodology:* *www.influxive.com/fdd-overview.html*
- *Feature-Driven Development™ (FDD™) and Agile Modeling*, Ambler S W: *www.agilemodeling.com/essays/fdd.htm*

Lean

- *Lean Primer*, Larman C & Vodde B (2009): *www.leanprimer.com/downloads/lean_primer.pdf*
- *Leading Lean Software Development: Results Are Not the Point,* Poppendieck.LLC (2009): *www.poppendieck.com/pdfs/llsd_intro.pdf*
- *Running Agile: A Practitioner's View to Lean and Agile:* *http://runningAgile.com/*

XP

- *Extreme Programming™: A Gentle Introduction:* *www.extremeprogramming.org*

Kanban

- *Kanban (overview): www.crisp.se/kanban*
- *Kanban and Scrum – making the most of both,* Kniberg H and Skarin M (2010): *www.infoq.com/minibooks/kanban-scrum-minibook*

RUP®

- *IBM Rational Unified Process® (RUP®):* *www-01.ibm.com/software/awdtools/rup*

- *Agile Modeling and the Rational Unified Process® (RUP®):* www.agilemodeling.com/essays/Agilemodelingrup.htm

EssUP

- *Essential Practices:* www.ivarjacobson.com/uploadedfiles/pages/knowledge_centre/resources/collateral/resources/essentialpractices2_brochure.pdf

AUP

- *The Agile Unified Process (AUP):* www.ambysoft.com/unifiedprocess/Agileup.html

Crystal

- *Crystal methodologies:* http://alistair.cockburn.us/crystal+methodologies

Selected Agile case studies

- *Agile Coaching in British Telecom*, Meadows L and Hanly S (2006): www.agilejournal.com/articles/columns/column-articles/144-Agile-coaching-in-british-telecom
- *Rolling Out Agile in a Large Enterprise,* Benefield G, Proceedings of the 41st Annual Hawaii International Conference on System Sciences (HICSS) (2008): http://dl.acm.org/citation.cfm?id=1334591

AUTHOR'S NOTE ON AGILE BUSINESS ANALYSIS RESOURCES

The resources listed in *Chapter 8: More Information on Agile* are primarily focused on the application of Agile approaches for project management and software development. There is currently very little published information specific to the role of the business analyst on Agile projects. People in the industry are, however, beginning to question whether the current Agile practices for identifying, analyzing, and delivering business user requirements are as effective as they could be.

There are a number of web pages, webinars, and slideshows that challenge whether Agile methods in their current form sufficiently address the business requirements of the organization, including:

- How business analysis is essential to Agile success *www.agilistapm.com/webinar-how-business-analysis-is-essential-to-Agile-success-627/*
- Requirements and Agile – Does it go hand in hand? *www.ibm.com/developerworks/mydeveloperworks/blogs/requirementsmanagement/entry/requirements_and_Agile_does_it_go_hand_in_hand_an_interview_with_Agile_business_analysis_expert_mary_gorman119?lang=en*

In particular, these sites are proposing that business analysts play a more active role in Agile work, bringing specialist skills to the team that software developers may lack. This discussion is currently taking place in web forums, webinars, and industry events, but there are few definitive resources available in the marketplace to comprehensively address this issue.

This indicates the Agile community is beginning to think critically about these practices, but the discussion needs more momentum.

For this reason, I have established a dedicated public website for these topics (*www.realproductivitygains.com*), to provide a foundation for communities of thought around Agile business concepts; a launching pad for discussion forums and blogs on business optimization; a place to download general business Agile tools; and a platform for business people to exchange and critique ideas on the successful application of Agile approaches.

ITG RESOURCES

IT Governance Ltd sources, creates and delivers products and services to meet the real-world, evolving IT governance needs of today's organisations, directors, managers and practitioners.

The ITG website (*www.itgovernance.co.uk*) is the international one-stop-shop for corporate and IT governance information, advice, guidance, books, tools, training and consultancy.

www.itgovernance.co.uk/project_governance.aspx is the information page on our website for Agile resources.

Other Websites

Books and tools published by IT Governance Publishing (ITGP) are available from all business booksellers and are also immediately available from the following websites:

www.itgovernance.eu is our euro-denominated website which ships from Benelux and has a growing range of books in European languages other than English.

www.itgovernanceusa.com is a US$-based website that delivers the full range of IT Governance products to North America, and ships from within the continental US.

www.itgovernanceasia.com provides a selected range of ITGP products specifically for customers in the Indian sub-continent.

www.itgovernance.asia delivers the full range of ITGP publications, serving countries across Asia Pacific. Shipping from Hong Kong, US dollars, Singapore dollars, Hong Kong dollars, New Zealand dollars and Thai baht are all accepted through the website.

Toolkits

ITG's unique range of toolkits includes the IT Governance Framework Toolkit, which contains all the tools and guidance that you will need in order to develop and implement an appropriate IT governance framework for your organisation.

For a free paper on how to use the proprietary Calder-Moir IT Governance Framework, and for a free trial version of the toolkit, see *www.itgovernance.co.uk/calder_moir.aspx*.

Training Services

IT Governance offers an extensive portfolio of training courses designed to educate information security, IT governance, risk management and compliance professionals. Our classroom and online training programmes will help you develop the skills required to deliver best practice and compliance to your organisation. They will also enhance your career by providing you with industry standard certifications and increased peer recognition. Our range of courses offer a structured learning path from Foundation to Advanced level in the key topics of information security, IT governance, business continuity and service management.

Our *Implementing IT Governance: Foundation and Principles* training course delivers introductory training to raise awareness, build knowledge and develop a complete understanding of IT governance and its implementation. It has been specifically designed to show delegates how to create a single integrated management framework that ensures that IT truly supports and delivers on all organisational strategies and objectives.

Full details of all IT Governance training courses can be found at *www.itgovernance.co.uk/training.aspx*.

Professional Services and Consultancy

The IT Governance Professional Services team can show you how to apply Agile concepts to the most complex development projects. Our expert consultants can guide and inspire you in the use of Agile, providing you with the practical techniques to improve delivery efficiencies, control your implementation costs, and meet your sales targets by building customer loyalty.

We believe that Agile Business Management is hard work and requires a cultural shift from the traditional business practices of hierarchical corporate structures, customer engagement, staff management, and work processes. We will show you the Agile methods that create flexibility and ensure adaptability to changing circumstances, accepting that nothing changes more than your Customer's needs. You will learn how to change from a traditional hierarchy towards self-empowered individuals and teams. In this way, you will develop engaged employees with the responsibility, accountability and authority to deliver to the Customer's Requirements, shaping and directing outcomes, while regularly delivering partial, though functional, products.

For more information about IT Governance: Consultancy and Training Services see:

www.itgovernance.co.uk/consulting.aspx.

Publishing Services

IT Governance Publishing (ITGP) is the world's leading IT-GRC publishing imprint that is wholly owned by IT Governance Ltd.

With books and tools covering all IT governance, risk and compliance frameworks, we are the publisher of choice for authors and distributors alike, producing unique and practical publications of the highest quality, in the latest formats available, which readers will find invaluable.

www.itgovernancepublishing.co.uk is the website dedicated to ITGP enabling both current and future authors, distributors, readers and other interested parties, to have easier access to more information. This allows ITGP website visitors to keep up to date with the latest publications and news.

Newsletter

IT governance is one of the hottest topics in business today, not least because it is also the fastest moving.

You can stay up to date with the latest developments across the whole spectrum of IT governance subject matter, including; risk management, information security, ITIL® and IT service management, project governance, compliance and so much more, by subscribing to ITG's core publications and topic alert emails.

Simply visit our subscription centre and select your preferences: *www.itgovernance.co.uk/newsletter.aspx*.

EU for product safety is Stephen Evans, The Mill Enterprise Hub, Stagreenan, Drogheda, Co. Louth, A92 CD3D, Ireland. (servicecentre@itgovernance.eu)

www.ingramcontent.com/pod-product-compliance
Lightning Source LLC
Chambersburg PA
CBHW061305220326
41599CB00026B/4734

* 9 7 8 1 8 4 9 2 8 5 0 4 9 *